WRITING ABOUT THE AMISH

A MEMOIR

BETH WISEMAN

PLEASE KEEP IN MIND THAT SOME OF THE PHOTOS IN THIS BOOK WERE TAKEN OVER A DECADE AGO, BEFORE CELL PHONES PROVIDED THE HIGHER RESOLUTIONS AVAILABLE NOW.

COPYRIGHT

Copyright © 2020 by Elizabeth Wiseman Mackey
ISBN 978-0997661095
All rights reserved.

No part of this book may be reproduced in any form or by any electronic or mechanical means, including information storage and retrieval systems, without written permission from the author, except for the use of brief quotations in a book review.

To protect the privacy of the Amish folks who helped me with research—some allowing me to take pictures—names and places have been changed to protect their privacy.

Every effort has been made by the author to ensure that the information contained in this book was correct as of press time. The author and publisher hereby disclaim and do not assume liability for any loss, damage, or disruption caused by errors or omissions, regardless of whether any errors or omissions results from negligence, accident, or any other cause. Readers are encouraged to verify any information contained in this book prior to taking any action on the information.

For rights and permissions, please contact:
Elizabeth Wiseman Mackey
P.O. Box 326
Fayetteville, TX 78940

ACCLAIM FOR BETH WISEMAN

Home All Along

"Beth Wiseman's novel will find a permanent home in every reader's heart as she spins comfort and prose into a stellar read of grace."

—Kelly Long, author of the Patch of Heaven series

Love Bears All Things

"Suggest to those seeking a more truthful, less saccharine portrayal of the trials of human life and the transformative growth and redemption that may occur as a result."

—Library Journal

Her Brother's Keeper

"Wiseman has created a series in which the readers have a chance to peel back all the layers of the Amish secrets."

—*RT Book Reviews*, 4 1/2 stars and July 2015 Top Pick!

"Wiseman's new launch is edgier, taking on the tough issues of mental illness and suicide. Amish fiction fans seeking something a bit more thought-provoking and challenging than the usual fare will find this series debut a solid choice."

—*Library Journal*

The Promise

"The story of Mallory in *The Promise* uncovers the harsh reality American women can experience when they follow their hearts into a very different culture. Her story sheds light on how Islamic society is totally different from the Christian marriage covenant between one man and one woman. This novel is based on actual events, and Beth reached out to me during that time. It was heartbreaking to watch those real-life events unfolding. I salute the author's courage, persistence, and final triumph in writing a revealing and inspiring story."

—Nonie Darwish, author of *The Devil We Don't Know*, *Cruel and Usual Punishment*, and *Now They Call Me Infidel*

"*The Promise* is an only too realistic depiction of an American young woman motivated by the best humanitarian impulses and naïve trust facing instead betrayal, kidnapping, and life-threatening danger in Pakistan's lawless Pashtun tribal regions. But the story offers as well a reminder just as realistic that love and sacrifice are never wasted and that the hope of a loving heavenly Father is never absent in the most hopeless of situations."

—Jeanette Windle, author of *Veiled Freedom* (2010 ECPA Christian Book Award/Christy Award finalist), *Freedom's Stand* (2012 ECPA Christian Book Award/Carol Award finalist), and *Congo Dawn* (2013 Golden Scroll Novel of the Year)

The House that Love Built

"This sweet story with a hint of mystery is touching and emotional. Humor sprinkled throughout balances the occasional seriousness. The development of the love story is paced perfectly so that the reader gets a real sense of the characters."

—*RT Book Reviews*, 4 stars

"[*The House that Love Built*] is a warm, sweet tale of faith renewed and families restored."

—*BookPage*

Need You Now

"Wiseman, best known for her series of Amish novels, branches out into a wider world in this story of family, dependence, faith, and small-town Texas, offering a character for every reader to relate to . . . With an enjoyable cast of outside characters, *Need You Now* breaks the molds of small-town stereotypes. With issues ranging from special education and teen cutting to what makes a marriage strong, this is a compelling and worthy read."

—*Booklist*

"Wiseman gets to the heart of marriage and family interests in a way that will resonate with readers, with an intricately written plot featuring elements that seem to be ripped from current headlines. God provides hope for Wiseman's characters even in the most desperate situations."

—*RT Book Reviews*, 4 stars

"You may think you are familiar with Beth's wonderful story-telling gift but this is something new! This is a story that will stay with you for a long, long time. It's a story of hope when life seems hopeless. It's a story of how God can redeem the seemingly unredeemable. It's a message the Church, the world needs to hear."

—Sheila Walsh, author of *God Loves Broken People*

"Beth Wiseman tackles these difficult subjects with courage and grace. She reminds us that true healing can only come by being vulnerable and honest before our God who loves us more than anything."

—Deborah Bedford, bestselling author of *His Other Wife*, *A Rose by the Door*, and *The Penny* (coauthored with Joyce Meyer)

The Land of Canaan Novels

"Wiseman's voice is consistently compassionate and her words flow smoothly."

—*Publishers Weekly* review of *Seek Me with All Your Heart*

"Wiseman's third Land of Canaan novel overflows with

romance, broken promises, a modern knight in shining armor, and hope at the end of the rainbow."

—*RT Book Reviews*

"In *Seek Me with All Your Heart*, Beth Wiseman offers readers a heartwarming story filled with complex characters and deep emotion. I instantly loved Emily, and eagerly turned each page, anxious to learn more about her past—and what future the Lord had in store for her."

—Shelley Shepard Gray, bestselling author of the Seasons of Sugarcreek series

"Wiseman has done it again! Beautifully compelling, *Seek Me with All Your Heart* is a heartwarming story of faith, family, and renewal. Her characters and descriptions are captivating, bringing the story to life with the turn of every page."

—Amy Clipston, bestselling author of *A Gift of Grace*

The Daughters of the Promise Novels

"Well-defined characters and story make for an enjoyable read."

—*RT Book Reviews* on *Plain Pursuit*

"A touching, heartwarming story. Wiseman does a particularly great job of dealing with shunning, a controversial Amish practice that seems cruel and unnecessary to outsiders . . . If you're a fan of Amish fiction, don't miss *Plain Pursuit*!"

—Kathleen Fuller, author of The Middlefield Family

This book is dedicated to all the Amish families who have shared their homes, information, and meals with me. I will be forever grateful for their willingness to assist me in writing stories that glorify God.

FROM THE AUTHOR

How could I have known that my first book—*Plain Perfect*—would set in motion a life-changing sequence of events that would forever change me as a person and alter my life in a way I never could have predicted? What started as a three-book series set in Lancaster County, Pennsylvania, morphed into a career that has spanned over a decade, so far. With over forty published stories, mostly novels and novellas centering around the Amish way of life, I have learned a lot from the Plain people. From that effort, I've tried to represent the Amish folks as accurately as possible, hoping to mentor to others about God's love and grace, without being preachy or over-the-top. My biggest surprise is, while writing the books, I've unknowingly been ministering to myself. I've gotten to know myself better through a stronger relationship with God, faced fears, acknowledged faults, and accepted God's grace and friendship into my life in a more personal way.

I set out to write one book that might possibly change

one life. I've received countless emails and letters suggesting that I have played a part in bettering another person's life and relationship with God. I'm wise enough to know this would be impossible without my Lord and Savior involved in every step of the process.

I have been abundantly blessed, and I try to never take that for granted. As I continue to write stories that I hope will inspire and entertain, I thank my readers for walking alongside me on this amazing journey. Above all else, I thank God for continuing to guide my hand and fill my head with stories that I hope will always glorify Him.

Throughout my journey among the Amish, I have been educated, entertained, and humbled. I've witnessed events that have dropped me to my knees in thanks and prayer. I have also found myself in situations that were humorous and surprising. I hope that you will enjoy traveling with me as I recall some of my favorite happenings with the Amish over the years.

May God's peace and blessings be present in all that you do and all that you are.

~ Beth Wiseman

ARE YOU AMISH?

Over the years, I've been asked quite a few times if I am Amish, despite the fact that I'm never wearing traditional Amish clothing. It seems to me that folks fall into one of three categories when it comes to the Plain people. They either know everything there is to know (or claim to), they are still studying and learning (like me), or they don't know anything at all about what it means to be Amish. I didn't know very much about the Amish, either, when I began writing books about these people who choose to live so differently than us.

Let's start with clothing. It's not universal when it comes to traditional Amish garb. Similar, yes, but not identical. The rules vary from state-to-state and even from district-to-district. Buttons on men's shirts might be allowed in one Amish community, but down the road in another district, it's a no-no. The same things apply to the style of clothing, distinguishing features of the prayer covering—*kapp* as they call it—length of dresses, whether or not dresses are pinned or not, colors allowed, etc.

Here are a few things I've been called out on over the years. Sometimes the reader was correct, and sometimes I was the one to politely set the inquirer straight.

- Reader: Your cover for *Plain Pursuit* is completely wrong. The boy has buttons on his shirt.
- Me: Panic. I was almost positive buttons were allowed. Sure enough, after researching and talking with a woman who used to be Amish, buttons are allowed in Paradise, Pennsylvania IN THAT DISTRICT. Further down the road, buttons not allowed.
- Reader: That woman's hair on the cover is parted on the side. All Amish women part their hair in the middle.
- Me: Again, I went back to my friend to ensure that parting a woman's hair on the side is allowed. It is.
- Reader: Your cover model has sculpted eyebrows.
- Me: Oops. The reader was correct. This was a book early in my career. You can probably identify which novel without me telling you.

And, last but not least. A BIG OOPS—My publisher blew up the cover of *Plain Pursuit* (book #2 in the Daughters or the Promise series) to use in an advertising campaign. Imagine my horror when I saw a wedding ring on the woman's third finger of her left hand. Amish folks do not wear wedding rings or jewelry of any kind. We didn't notice it until the cover was blown up, so the ring was removed, and in all future editions there is no wedding ring. If you own *Plain Pursuit*, look closely at the woman in the background. If you see a wedding ring on her finger, then you have a first edition copy of the book.

So, what would I look like if I were Amish? Turn the page to see for yourself.

Plain Paradise

BETH WISEMAN

BEST-SELLING AUTHOR OF *PLAIN PERFECT*

PUBLIC AFFECTION

Readers of Amish fiction know that public affection is frowned upon. As an author in this genre, I know the Plain people are modest and don't openly display physical endearment. Well, I guess I forgot.

A friend and I traveled to Lancaster County to do research. We met with several Amish families, and we dined in an Amish home that had housed five generations. The owner was happy to have us stay after the meal to answer questions. She was a lovely woman, very helpful, warm and congenial. We're from Texas, so hugging her when we left that evening felt as natural as breathing. Texans hug everyone. It wasn't awkward at all, and she returned the embrace.

On the day we were scheduled to return home, my friend and I wanted to tell this sweet Amish woman goodbye. We attended an event where we knew she would be. I honestly can't remember the venue. That was over a decade ago, and I've slept since then. But, two things stick out in my mind. First, we were the only non-Amish people there. We found our Amish friend standing outside a building surrounded by a group of other Amish women. Excited, we rushed toward her, excusing ourselves for interrupting, but happy to have found her among the crowd.

After thanking her profusely for spending time with us, I threw my arms around her. I thought I felt her arms tense at her sides, but before I had time to process her reaction, I'd stepped aside. My bubbly friend was next, wrapping the woman in a big bear hug. It was then that I noticed the expressions of the women in the group, their surprised gazes ping-ponging from one to the other. And the woman we hugged turned three shades of red.

I'm not going to say that all of the Plain people resist hugging in public. But I saw and felt a level of unease firsthand, so now I don't hug my Amish friends and acquaintances, privately or otherwise. My intent is to always respect their ways, and I don't want to cross any lines. Perhaps I should have known better. I'd heard about their resistance to any type of public affection. But, I suppose, I was thinking more about romantic kisses, and things like that. Thank goodness I didn't kiss her on the cheek too.

THE TOWN OF INTERCOURSE

You can't visit Lancaster County, Pennsylvania, without wandering into the town of Intercourse. This community in the heart of Amish Country was founded in 1754, but it was originally named Cross Keys, which was the name of a local tavern. There are various theories about why the town was renamed in 1814, but perhaps those are to be debated in another book.

When I wrote my first Amish book, *Plain Perfect*, my editor asked me if we could remove the town of Intercourse, citing that it was a distraction while reading the manuscript. At the time, there were only a few authors writing Amish fiction, and the genre was growing, but it hadn't risen to the popularity it is now. I explained to my editor that the town of Intercourse was as popular as the towns of Bird-In-Hand and Paradise, to omit it would be an omission of authenticity to the area. She ultimately allowed the use of Intercourse.

While dining with an Amish family over ten years

ago, I wrongly assumed that everyone knew that the word 'intercourse' wasn't just the name of a town. Following a lovely meal, I fell into a casual conversation with an Amish teenage girl. She was interested in my books. I explained to her how my editor had originally wanted me to omit the town of Intercourse from *Plain Perfect*.

"Why would she want you to do that? Intercourse is very popular with the tourists," she told me.

I started to explain to her about the meaning of the word, but when her eyes widened and I felt her mother's eyes on me, I backtracked in a big way. It became obvious that this innocent teenager did not know where I was headed with my explanation so I finagled my way out of an embarrassing moment for everyone.

Now, that might seem far-fetched, but I have another story that supports the naivety of the young people in Amish communities. I was told by a reliable source that a young couple visited their doctor, concerned because the wife had not yet become pregnant. They explained how they had been sleeping together for months without being able to conceive a child. After further evaluation, the doctor learned that the couple had been doing exactly what they said—*sleeping* together—as in closing your eyes and catching some shuteye. True story. You're probably thinking about how these young people grew up on a farm and were surely educated as to how the reproduction process works. Apparently not.

Pictured on the next page (left to right) are Beth, editor Natalie Hanemann, and bestselling author Kelly Long.

INTERCOURSE
FORMERLY "CROSS KEYS"
FROM A NOTED OLD TAVERN STAND
FOUNDED
1754

AN AMISH RESTROOM TO REMEMBER

I've been in a lot of Amish homes, shops, and bakeries. But one trip to the ladies room in an Amish bakery tops my list.

A friend took me to a bakery where they still use wood ovens for baking. As always, these Plain people were courteous, and the food was amazing. It was definitely an off-the-beaten-path place out in the middle of nowhere. A family member went there often, and she took me along on one of my trips to Indiana. I bought the best fried pies I've ever tasted. I even based my story —*Loaves of Love*, from *An Amish Christmas Bakery* collection—on this very unique bakery. They sold homemade pies and loaves of bread. The aroma was heavenly, and it was so fun watching the ladies pulling baked goods out of a wood oven.

After we had been there a while, I asked if I could use the restroom. A sweet young Amish woman pointed me toward a door that led to a short hallway with another door at the end. I thanked her and made my way there.

Then I just stood there and looked at the bench where folks did their business. I stayed in there long enough to pretend I was utilizing the facility. But I just couldn't do it. Maybe it was the fact that there were paper towels instead of toilet paper. But I think mostly my resistance was due to the two makeshift holes roughly cut into the bench. I honestly thought I might get splinters if I sat down.

After I'd spent what I considered a sufficient amount of time in the tiny room, I exited. A young Amish woman was waiting for me and directed me to a sink. She pumped warm water for me to wash my hands, and she had a warm towel folded over her arm for drying my hands.

I thanked her. I bought lots of goodies that day. Then we scurried to go find another bathroom. Did I mention we were out in the middle of nowhere?

See pictures on next few pages.

Mixing business with pleasure.
Beth and her grandson in
Montgomery, Indiana.

THE BIG SPILL

The name Allen Arnold is well known in the world of Christian publishing. He started the fiction program for Thomas Nelson Publishers, now a division of HarperCollins Christian Publishing. Even though he has gone on to pursue other endeavors, he is still actively involved with Christian publishing and ministry. He's even written a book—*The Story of With*. Check it out. Wise words written by a wise man.

I can't remember what year it was, but I was early into my career when 'the big spill' occurred. Allen was my publisher and boss. He was larger than life, but despite his charm and easy-going ways, he made me nervous as a cat whose tail was loitering under a rocking chair.

I do remember where 'the big spill' happened—following a conference in Indianapolis, Indiana. I don't remember which hotel, but it doesn't matter. As many times as I've reenacted one of the most embarrassing moments in my life, I would recognize the lobby bar right away.

The mishap occurred following the big awards ceremony for the coveted Carol Awards, presented by ACFW (American Christian Fiction Writers). I don't remember if I was a finalist, winner, or neither that year. Time has left me with only one recollection of that event.

Allen and I were talking about my career, and there was even mention of a new contract coming soon. It seemed a margarita was in order. My agent (at the time) handed me a tall glass. In my defense, it was too tall to house a margarita overfilled with ice. But I set the glass on the small cocktail table. I didn't sit down when Allen did. I was too busy talking with my hands and rambling on about what I wanted to write. We were still dressed in our fancy party clothes. Worth a mention since his clothes wouldn't be party worthy for long.

I hadn't even taken one sip of that drink when my hand met with the full glass, toppling it onto his side of the table, with the entire greenish-colored beverage landing in Mr. Arnold's lap.

His jaw dropped (aside from the shock, I'm sure it was plenty cold). Everyone around us gasped. I wanted the floor to crack open and swallow me up. My agent simply said, "I'll get you another drink."

When the floor didn't swallow me up, I apologized profusely as bystanders found napkins to offer the ever-gracious Allen Arnold, who insisted he was fine. He looked like he had wet his pants, so I know he was just being kind.

After returning home, having left a portion of my

dignity in Indianapolis, I decided to send Allen a gift, an apology of sorts. I knew he was a big fan of hot sauce, so I chose a lovely gift set that included hot sauce and snacks. I enclosed this note: *Here is a little something hot to make up for the cold I dumped in your lap.*

His response? He thanked me for the gift and said, *"But I will never let you live this down."* And he hasn't. The story has been told many times. I've heard it from people I'd never met before. To be fair, I've told the story lots of times too.

When I dined with Allen in a group not long after the event, before I ordered a drink (of water, again in too tall of a glass with an excessive amount of ice), I passed a package to him. He was seated at the opposite end of the table from me—a seat he surely chose on purpose. My gift to him was one of those orange rain ponchos you might take on a camping trip. He didn't put it on. Guess he felt safe so far away from me.

The photo on the next page is of Allen and me years later. Gotta love him.

He still makes me nervous. I think I only make him nervous if there are tall drinks nearby.

Beth and Allen Arnold

DO THE PLAIN PEOPLE READ AMISH BOOKS?

This is a question I've posed to several Amish women. "Do you read Amish books?" While some of the ladies have confessed that they don't understand the special interest we have in their lifestyle, they did admit to reading Amish-themed novels. I've been told this type of reading is not disallowed, but that most bishops don't encourage it. But, as long as the chosen Amish books (and other genres) are clean and wholesome, no one makes a fuss.

Several mothers told me they screen all the books their preteen and teenage daughters read. Every time I have given one of my novels or a novella collection to anyone Amish, they've been thrilled. And most of the time I leave with a gift after my visits with these lovely people. I've been given cookbooks and yummy baked goods, just to name a couple of items.

The Amish also utilize libraries, and on a recent trip to Montgomery, Indiana, I ran across the tiniest library ever. There was even a copy of my very first book, *Plain Perfect.*

This is the entire library.
That little cutie is my grandson. The puppy just
just wandered in.

Plain Perfect!

EVEN THE MEN READ

The photo on the next page was taken with this man's permission. Although, to respect his privacy I have blurred his face.

He isn't reading one of my Amish books. Instead, he is reading one of my Texas contemporary novels, *Need You Now*.

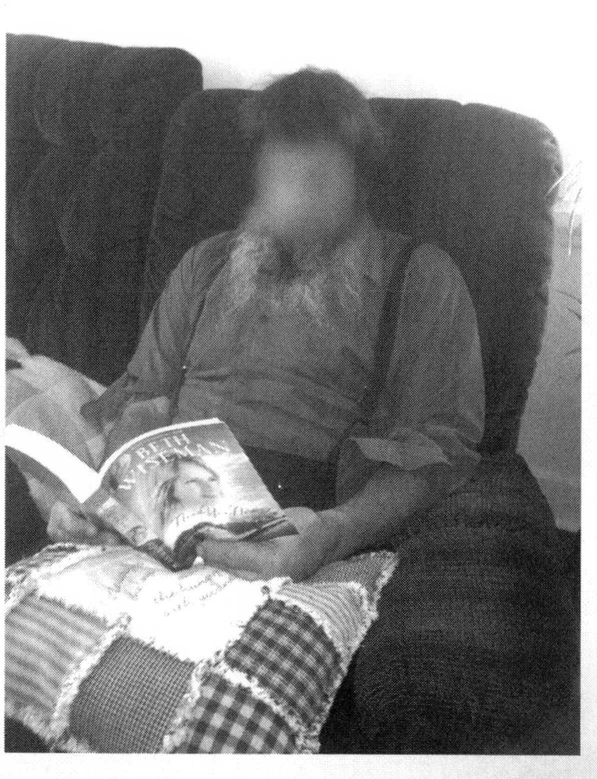

THE GRAY AREAS

Most people—especially readers of Amish fiction—know quite a bit about the Old Order Amish. They don't use electricity, although some utilize propane and solar panels. Phones—home and/or cell—are forbidden in some communities, but allowed for business purposes in most districts. Smart phones (with Internet, etc.) aren't allowed within any Amish communities I've visited. Teenagers are allowed a running around period (*rumpschpringe*) when they turn sixteen years old. It's a time for them to bend the rules and decide for sure if they want to be baptized into the Amish faith. And all but about five percent choose baptism.

We are familiar with the Amish dress code, which also varies from district to district. The women wear prayer coverings (*kapps*), and the Plain people speak Pennsylvania Dutch as their first language. Children (*kinner*) don't learn English until they start school when they are five years old. I could go on and on about Amish customs, traditions, and their rules (*Ordnung*), but what about the gray areas? Here are a few gray areas I have stumbled upon:

- I once asked an Amish woman how an Amish owned restaurant could get by with using electricity at their place of business, but not at home. She explained that the restaurant was co-owned by a non-Amish partner, making it acceptable to have electricity. *Gray area.*

- A lovely Amish woman invited me to her home. Her family had moved from a farm and into a house in town. There were other Amish nearby, comingling with the non-Amish (*English*, as they are referred to). Two of her sons are in that five-percent of adolescents who chose not to be baptized into the faith. As such, they can remain close with their family. In the case of this family, the sons remained in the house with their parents. A shunning only occurs when a baptized member of a community breaks the rules. As I visited with Sarah, there wasn't any electricity, and she showed me her wringer washing machine. When it came time for me to fly back to Texas, she loaded me up with yummy snacks to take on the plane. I was still early into my Amish research at this time. I asked her if it would be all right if I wrote to her, maybe with follow-up questions. She leaned close and whispered, "You can just email me." Of course, I asked her how that was possible. She said that since her sons chose not to be baptized, they had electricity on the other side of the house, which included a computer and email. LOL. *Gray area.*

- Most people know that the Amish do not like their pictures taken, for religious reasons, and I'm sure it's annoying to have tourists in your face all the time. But I've had my picture taken with an Amish woman who had no problem posing for the photo.

So, as with any of us, rules are sometimes interpreted differently, or the person has chosen to bend the rules. But, the majority of Amish folks I've met do not want their picture taken.

WHEN CHARACTERS BECOME REAL

While I was writing my first series—The Daughters of the Promise—I was fortunate to make friends with a woman in Lancaster County, Pennsylvania. At first, Barbie helped me via phone calls and email. She would read my manuscripts and make corrections, which was particularly helpful because she came from an Amish upbringing. Her parents had been Old Order, then converted to Beachy Amish (less conservative Order), and that is how Barbie grew up. She later joined a non-denominational Christian church. Over time, we became good friends, and I was able to visit her several times in Paradise, a town in Lancaster County. At the time, Barbie and her husband owned a bed and breakfast, which is where I stayed during my visits. Barbie was instrumental in putting me in touch with some lovely Amish folks who spent time with me and educated me about their way of life.

I have used the names of friends in my books before. It's always fun for them to be reading along and see their name used for a character. I didn't think too much about it when I included Barbie's name in several of the Daughters of the Promise books. I also used the name of the bed and breakfast that Barbie and her husband were running at the time. Barbie's role in the stories was that she was a driver for the Amish. As others had said, she thought it was fun to be mentioned in the books.

Then it went from fun to hilarious when the lines between fiction and truth began to blur. Folks started showing up at her B&B and thought she actually drove the Amish around from place to place. Barbie had plenty of Amish friends, but she wasn't a driver for hire as portrayed in my books. I'd just used the name of her bed and breakfast, along with her name, for fun. I thought it might boost her business, even though her B&B didn't need any help from me. It was a lovely and popular place. But she got a kick out of the fact that readers assumed she was, in fact, the person in the books, right down to her occupation as hired driver.

Choosing a name can be a long process, at least for me. And sometimes character names change several times throughout the writing process until I land on one that fits. In Barbie's case, it was fun and we had some good laughs about it. But, other times, I've chosen names strictly because the name seemed to suit the character, with no other relevancy.

But it's hard to choose a name that isn't somehow associated with someone in your life, even it was unintentional. Here are a few comments (paraphrased from memory) when I've used someone's first name.

— Hey, I would never act like that.

— Why did you make me a bad guy?

— I'm alive, not dead!

— Why did you kill me off?

— You killed my bird! (from long time BFF Renee' when I named a parrot after her parrot—Elvis. The bird died in the story, but was given an elaborate funeral complete with a fancy coffin and formal burial.

— That's not the color of my hair.

Most of the time, I never had that person in mind when I wrote the story. It was just a good name for my character. Having said that, if I'm writing about a bad guy (or gal), I try to reach as far away as I can from anyone I know, lol.

However, I never received any complaints from Chloe, my Labrador, or other pets I've included in my books.

THE ACCIDENT

Early in my career, I tried to find out as much as I could about the Plain people. I researched, made friends in Amish Country, and was blessed by the way God blew open doors of opportunity to help me get started.

One of the first things I did during a trip to Lancaster County was to pay for a ride in an Amish buggy—the type of buggy that was built more as a tour-bus buggy than what an authentic Amish ride would actually be like. And the driver may or may not have been Amish, even though he donned the traditional Amish clothing, hat, and beard.

As I got to know some Amish families and began getting invited into their homes, I mentioned that I'd never been on a 'real' buggy ride. A kind Amish woman, whom I'd gotten to know fairly well, offered to take me on a ride. It was nearing dark, but I was thrilled and didn't want to miss out on an opportunity, especially since my private tour would take me through one of the popular covered bridges.

Our journey also took us along Lincoln Highway, a busy road that runs right through the heart of Paradise—a popular town in Lancaster County. And, sure enough, darkness fell, and my heart rate soared as cars whizzed by us. My Amish friend (we'll call her Mary) kept the horse in a steady trot and didn't seem the least bit phased by the busy highway at nighttime. I reminded myself that she travels this way all the time.

A few things ran through my mind. I'd already been told that many of the horses the Amish use to pull the buggies are retired racehorses—and when they hear a fire alarm, the animals relate the loud noise as the 'start' of a race and often take off at top speed pulling the buggy.

As we drove near the fire station, my chest tightened, and I prayed there wouldn't be any fires that evening. Just the same, my stomach clenched most of the ride. I think I would have enjoyed the trip a lot more if it had been daylight and if the last leg of the journey hadn't been alongside a busy highway.

I breathed a sigh of relief when we pulled onto Mary's road. After she slowed the buggy to a stop, the conversation went something like this:

"Wow, that was so different than the buggy rides offered to tourists." Actually, it was a lot more bumpy than I would have predicted. "Thank you so much."

"*Ya, ya.* You're very welcome." Mary shook her head. "I'm just glad everything went okay."

Huh? Why wouldn't it have? Maybe she wasn't used to driving at night after all. I just smiled. We were safe.

My stomach was beginning to settle down, and my pulse was returning to normal. I thanked her again.

She nodded, then smiled at me. "I feel *gut* about that little ride. It's the first time I've been back in the buggy since the accident."

I sat taller, swallowing hard. "The accident?"

"*Ya.*" She looked at me, then chuckled. "I've rigged a horse to a buggy hundreds of times, but a neighbor was chatting with me, and I guess I got distracted."

I don't remember the exact lingo she used, but basically she said that she didn't have the horse and buggy hooked up properly when she got in the seat and prepared to give the horse a gentle flick of the reins. But the reins, the horse, the buggy—it wasn't set up correctly, in a way that the horse could do whatever he wanted without her having any control with the reins.

"He just took off." Mary made a sweep of her hand as she shook her head again. "I just had to hold on and hope for the best."

My jaw dropped. I was quite sure that if I'd heard this story prior to my authentic buggy ride, I would have opted out.

Mary sighed. "Eventually, I was thrown from the buggy. I got pretty banged up too." She listed her injuries, and while I was sympathetic to the pain and suffering she must have gone through, I was also thanking God repeatedly that we had arrived back at Mary's house in one piece. I exited the buggy pretty quickly.

There were other buggy rides for me, but none of them were at night or near a busy highway.

A SPECIAL COVER SHOOT

Most of the covers for my books have included a cover shoot with a professional model. Sometimes, a brilliant designer at the publishing house builds the cover utilizing software for that purpose.

For my book—*His Love Endures Forever* (Book 2 in the Land of Canaan series)—the cover was being shot in Colorado because the book's setting is Colorado. My husband and I have good friends in Colorado and were excited to spend some time with them. But I had also made a suggestion to my publishing team that I was very excited about.

I realize how blessed I am to have had my BFF for over forty years. Renee' Bissmeyer carries in her memories the diary of my life. She is my soul mate, best friend, and the one person who would 'bury the body', lol. During the planning stages of the cover for *His Love Endures Forever*, Renee's daughter had recently been signed with a major modeling agency. Since my publisher hired models through an agency, I asked if they would consider Renee's daughter—Christie—as the cover model. After seeing pictures of Christie, who is gorgeous inside and out, they agreed to have her on the cover.

My husband and I flew to Colorado, and after visiting with our friends, we picked Christie up at the Denver airport a few days later. Our friend Sherry was also able to attend. Wow. It was a special day. I'd never been to a cover shoot. They take a ton of pictures with varying poses and outfits (Amish, in this case). But be still my heart. The thought of having my best friend's daughter on the cover of a book, a beautiful woman whom I'd known since she was born . . . There are no words. It was a very special occasion for me, Renee', and Christie. And I loved that my husband was able to be there, along with our friend, Sherry.

And the cover of *His Love Endures Forever* is one of my favorites, for the lovely design and fabulous photography. But also for the beauty I know is in Christie's heart. Love you, Christie, and thank you.

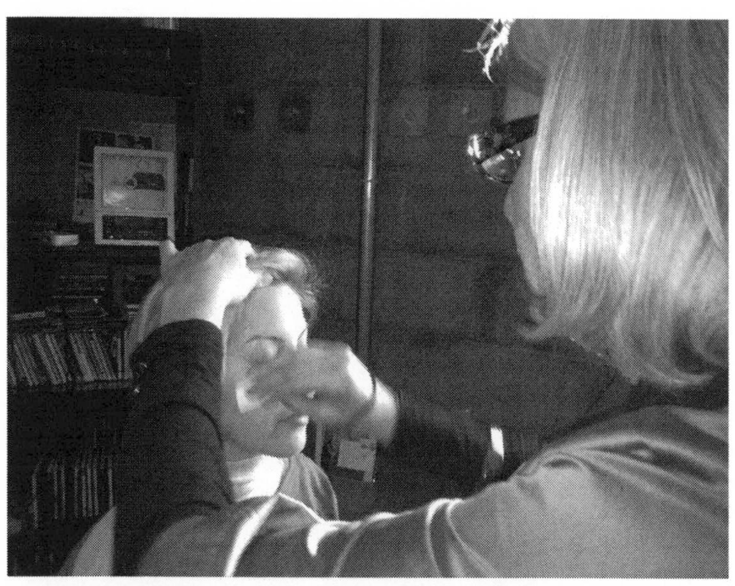

Beautiful Christie!

The End Result

AND ALONG CAME JANET

I was about a year into my publishing journey—roughly ten years ago—when I realized I needed help. Even though I had left my job as a newspaper reporter and was writing full-time from home, I couldn't keep up. In addition to writing, revising, and proofing my novels, there were a ton of backend responsibilities that needed handling. Social media was on the rise, specifically Facebook, and the promotional aspect of writing began to weigh me down.

And, it wasn't just online responsibilities that bogged me down. I needed someone to keep me on task, help me schedule events, assist at book signings, and a host of other things related to writing for a living. So I ran an ad in our local newspaper. I offered an hourly rate mostly targeted toward a high school student, and I only needed someone part-time.

I interviewed several applicants. One young lady might have worked, but there was going to be considerable training involved, and this high school student would be off to college the following year. Another sweet girl met me at McDonalds with her toddler, which I'd told her was fine. But, it was easy to see that she had her hands full already, and I worried if she could fully commit. I wouldn't have been able to when my children were young, so I'm not placing any fault on her situation. There were others, but no one seemed to fit.

Then along came Janet. She was different from the young people I'd spoken with. We set a date to meet for lunch. For starters, she was late. Anyone who knows me well is aware that I am a stickler for punctuality. I'd honestly written her off before she arrived. I know that sounds harsh (and I probably shouldn't admit it), but it's the truth.

Janet was a sweet retired woman, and we had several mutual acquaintances. She was soft-spoken and didn't come across as very confident. (Boy, howdy, was I wrong on that first impression). Janet didn't know much about social media platforms other than Facebook, had never set up or maintained a website (which was an attribute I had been looking for in a student assistant), and she didn't know a thing about the book industry, although she was a lovely person. But the old cliché that God works in mysterious ways was definitely in play the day I met Janet Murphy.

That evening, I told my husband that I'd struck out again. I just wasn't finding the person I had pictured in my mind. I felt a bit defeated. Then I received an email from Janet. She basically listed all the reasons that I didn't need a student assistant. She had valid points to consider.

Then she listed all the reasons that I should hire her. That meek, quiet, soft-spoken person I'd met earlier wasn't who leapt from the pages of the email. This woman was confident, clearly educated (I have horrible grammar), and she went as far as to say that she would make herself irreplaceable as my assistant. THEN . . . wait for it . . .

Janet closed her email by saying that she was the person I needed to choose for the position, but she was not going to do it for what I was offering as an hourly wage. Then she presented the dollar amount she was willing to work for.

I actually laughed out loud, then read the email to my husband (what I wouldn't do to still have that email). Our conversation went something like this:

HUBBY – "Wow."

ME – "I know. Can you believe that?"

HUBBY – "She's bold. You gotta give her that."

ME – I got very quiet. Something niggled me in a way I didn't quite recognize. I know now that it was God, but at the time, I just had a gut feeling about this woman. I turned to my husband and smiled. "I'm going to hire her," I told him.

And I did.

Ten years later, Janet is everywhere, behind the scenes handling all the things that wouldn't get handled if she weren't onboard. Assistant isn't an accurate word to describe Janet. She's a marketing guru, continually educates herself in an ever-changing industry, and she coordinates promotions with my street team, Wiseman's Warriors. Janet reminds me about events, dates to remember (even birthdays), deadlines I'd surely miss otherwise, and generally keeps me on task.

Mostly, Janet is my voice of reason. I'm an idea person, and occasionally I have some good ones. But, more often than not, I get hyped up about something I have no business doing. Here's an example:

ME – "Hey, Janet, I think I'm going to open a bookstore on the square in town. Some retail space became available."

JANET – (insert heavy sigh). "No. You're not." Then she listed all the reasons why this was a bad idea. The largest of those being lack of time. And she was right all across the board.

So, in closing, I'll say this: Janet is, indeed (without a doubt), irreplaceable to me, and she wears many writing-related hats. She's everything an author needs in an assistant—again, not a good word to describe this amazing woman.

But, back to how God works in mysterious ways. How could I have ever known that Janet would become so much more than someone who works for me? God planted the seed for friendship that day we met, and it has continued to blossom over the past decade. Janet's soft-spoken nature calms my often wild and out of control creative mind. That same disposition carries over into my personal life. She has a calming effect on me when there are challenges unrelated to business. But, I would be lax if I didn't mention that Janet is also one of the funniest people I know. Her dry sense of humor has had me crying from laughter on many occasions. We've made memories we'll carry for a lifetime. I would be remiss if I didn't include this snippet in this book.

Yep. God knew what He was doing that day Janet arrived late at the restaurant. But as is His way, I couldn't foresee into the future. He knew what was best for me, and He gifted me with a person who would help me organize my life in a way that I could continue to write stories that glorify Him. But He also blessed me with a dear friend for life.

So, Janet . . . here's to another decade or two . . . maybe more, God willing.

Beth and Janet

THE UPS—AND THE "DOWNS"

I'm tall. Depending on which doctor's assistant measures my height, I'm somewhere between 5'8" and 5'10". It seems to me they should be able to pin that down, but that's a discussion for another time. However, I enjoyed (past tense, explanation further down) wearing heels, and I have a love relationship with shoes.

On a trip to New York City, I wanted to dress the part, so I wore a modest, if not a bit shorter than usual, dress. Of course, I matched my outfit with a lovely pair of wedge heels. Not stilettos, just nice and safe four-inch wedges, which propelled me to over six-feet tall by all varying calculations. I was traveling alone from Texas and meeting my agent (at the time) at the Waldorf Astoria Hotel. I was excited to be in New York City, and as I hurriedly retrieved my carry-on bag, then made my way down the Jetway, I fell off those nice and safe wedges I'd chosen.

It happened fast. I couldn't tell you if my foot gave

out, my ankle twisted, if I tripped, or if someone pushed me. (I don't think anyone pushed me. I'm just throwing that into the story as a remote possibility to make me seem less clumsy).

However it happened, I was face down in a less than flattering way with a herd of people behind me. Did I mention that shorter than usual dress? I still cringe at the visual.

Just to note—when a tall person goes down, wearing four-inch heels (even if they are wedges), getting up is no easy task. It took two big, strong men to get me to my feet. I quickly thanked them, left my wounded ego behind, and carried on. I ignored the blood running down my leg until I'd snagged a taxi. Getting a cab in NYC is also a tale for another time.

The taxi driver obliged my request for a napkin after almost having forty-two wrecks while he weaved through traffic, opening every compartment in the cab to find something for my busted knee. He finally handed me a used brown napkin that looked like it came from a used McDonald's Happy Meal. It was hard to differentiate what was blood and what was ketchup.

But, finally, I was at the Waldorf. I exited the cab and forgot about my knee. I took in the lavish hotel and my surroundings in Manhattan. I felt like *'That Girl'*. For younger readers, *That Girl* was a 1960s sitcom about an actress who moves to New York City to make it big. I was there to attend an awards gala. One of my books was a finalist for the prestigious Audie Award.

The Audio Publishers Association honors the best books in audio publishing by hosting an award ceremony.

This honor is mostly for the narrators of the audiobooks, delegated by category. But there are also some authors sprinkled throughout the crowd, and a nomination gives the book exposure. Twice I've been an invited guest in New York City, where the gala was being held the two times one of my books was a finalist for the prestigious award.

I hadn't even made it up two steps to the hotel when a nice older man had me by the elbow. How lovely, I thought. I'm being escorted by one of the staff into the hotel. Once inside, he rushed me along and guided me to a sitting area, nearly out of sight, I might add. After I sat down, I saw blood trailing down my leg and pooling atop my lovely wedged shoe. The nice man, in uniform, pressed a starched white handkerchief—nothing like the napkin from the cab driver—against my bloody knee. I'd honestly forgotten about it at this point.

The doorman left me but quickly returned with bandages and ointment, then he doctored my knee. Apparently, the Waldorf doesn't care for patrons entering the building trailing blood along the way. Understandable.

I was unaffected, slouched back into the chair, and asked the man if I could take a picture of him tending to my knee. He smiled and said it would be okay. I thanked him, while trying to be mindful of my shorter-than-usual dress, and snapped several pictures.

Oh, how I wish I had one of those photos to share with you. But, alas, I have no idea where they are since that was nearly a decade ago. But the visual will remain with me forever.

I've given up wearing my heels, even the ones that look deceivingly safe. I quit *wearing* them, but I still have them. They are on display in my closet. Who knows, perhaps I'll dust off a pair for a special occasion. And someday, I'll award them to a person who will appreciate them.

Someday.

THE RED SUITCASE

Only a handful of people know there is a red suitcase mentioned in every Beth Wiseman book. In the beginning, the publisher and I tried to keep it a secret, thinking we would offer a prize to anyone who could guess what tangible item was in all of my books. But, it's been over a decade, and we haven't done that. So, I think it's okay to go public and explain how the red suitcase came to be.

It was a casual conversation among girlfriends, and I honestly can't remember enough about our discussion to even paraphrase it well. But, it was decided on our porch on a sunny afternoon that each book would have a red suitcase. My editors have all known not to edit that detail out of any books, and they usually put a smiley face next to it while revising the manuscript. My current editor usually writes, "There it is!"

I am 99% sure I haven't missed an inclusion in all of my stories. But, here's a challenge for you! If you find any book I've written—Amish or otherwise—that doesn't have a red suitcase, email me, and I'll send you a signed copy of any book you choose (that I have in stock, lol).

Happy Reading!

In my mind, this is the type of red suitcase I see.

IT'S NOT ALL GLITZ AND GLAMOUR

Back in the day, long before I published my first book, there were lavish book release parties. Authors were ushered around and introduced conceptually like movie stars, high profile figures who had created a work of art that catapulted them to near-stardom. At least that's what I've heard.

While I'm sure some authors enjoy that type of glitz and glamour, I assure you, most of us do not.

We have a marketing team and a publicist who work hard to get our books prime placement in retail outlets, secure blogging opportunities, arrange Facebook chats, set up radio interviews and speaking engagements, and a host of other team-related efforts. But there is no party, no champagne, no need to buy a brand new cocktail dress.

Authors are expected to work hard promoting our books via our social media platforms, networking with industry professionals, nurturing our treasured readership, and being mindful that these efforts are necessary to ensure the book gets off to a good start.

But, even though we don't get a fancy release party, there are times when we do get to enjoy a bit of that glitz and glamour.

American Christian Fiction Writers (ACFW) holds an annual conference to honor novels in relevant categories. On the evening of the awards banquet, authors, agents, publishers, guests, and the media gather for a wonderful meal and the winners of the Carol Awards are revealed. Things get a little fancy for the event. I've been fortunate to be a finalist several times, and twice I've won the coveted award. There is also an award for Agent of the Year. On the following page is a photo when both my agent and I scored a win in the same year. I won the Carol Award, and Natasha Kern won Agent of the Year.

Another lavish gathering is when the Audie Awards are presented. That trip to NYC was one of the few times I shook the dust from a pair of high heels.

Beth and her agent, Natasha Kern, at ACFW Awards Ceremony

Beth and her sister-in-law, Melody, at the Waldorf Astoria New York

ODD PLACES TO HAVE BOOK SIGNINGS

When we think of book signing locations, libraries and bookstores come to mind. But when my first series—Daughters of the Promise—released, I wanted to think outside of the box. I live in a small town with few opportunities nearby to market my books, so I had to find places where people gathered when it wasn't convenient for me to travel far from home.

It's amazing the places people will buy books! A liquor store, for example. Now, keep in mind, this is a family-owned and operated place in a small town. It wasn't like I was selling Christian books at a big chain. I know the owners, and they are wonderful people. When they asked if I wanted to do a book signing at their place, I decided I better get permission from my publisher, lol. They gave me a thumb's up once I explained about the venue.

I noticed right away that it seemed to be mostly men coming into the store on their way home from work. Mostly, they were toting a six-pack of beer. Hmm . . .

these were not the type of people who typically read my books, so I needed an angle, a marketing tool. And once I landed on the right phrase, it worked every single time.

"Hi, how are you? Would you like to buy a signed copy of my book to take home to your wife?" Then I'd eye the six-pack ever so slightly and smile.

Every one of those men bought a book, and somewhere there is a picture floating around of a man holding his beer while I sign his wife's book. Over the years, the photo has gone missing. But the memory remains.

I probably sold the most books ever at a car dealership. That could be because my husband worked there and the owners talked it up. Whatever the reason, people came! And they bought books. Some folks even browsed cars. It was a fun event, and I'm thankful to Tommy and Karen Brasher for hosting me at their dealership.

My publisher at the time talked enthusiastically about the places I found to sell books. He would tell other authors to be creative about venues, like Beth Wiseman.

Ha! I was just a small town girl trying to sell books anywhere I could. Still am.

WE DON'T SMOKE

After my editor learned about a trend in Colorado, we decided I should write about the Amish who were migrating to the San Luis Valley. According to various sources, the Plain people were moving from Pennsylvania, Iowa, Ohio, Indiana, New York, and other states, purchasing available land that was less expensive. Particularly in Pennsylvania, the Amish were also running out of property with each new generation.

Since we have good friends in Colorado that we visit as often as we can, my husband and I decided to combine a little work and play. We traveled to Baily, Colorado to spend time with Tim and Sherry, then made plans to travel to the San Luis Valley.

Most readers familiar with the Amish genre know that things differ from state to state, and even from district to district within a state. This was most apparent when we visited two Amish families in the San Luis Valley. The first family lived in a rural area and had a dozen or so children. I'm not sure I've ever been in an Amish home when I wasn't offered cookies so that one constant seems to be prevalent across the miles.

What felt different about this first visit in San Luis Valley is the way the children stared at us as if we were from another planet. Yes, there were cookies. Yes, the family members who were present were very hospitable. But we were an oddity among them based on the curious expressions from the kiddos. The mom showed me how to use a loom, which is a device used to weave tapestry and cloth. And I saw an animal skin drying outside. It was the first time I learned that the Amish hunt. It was a question that hadn't come up in my visits to Pennsylvania.

The family owned a small general store, and I was told that the community was new and still establishing itself. We had a lovely visit, and I was told about the challenges of growing and harvesting in that area since they didn't have very much frost-free weather each year.

I had no idea that my next visit with another family would bring forth a reprimand. Miles away, there was another community newly settled. When we drove up to their driveway, I knew we were in for a completely different experience. The house looked brand new, and for lack of a better word, appeared fancy—inside and out. Although, this woman seemed guarded as she spoke to us, Lydia graciously answered my questions.

The most important take away from the first part of our conversation was when I asked her who set the community rules. If Amish families were arriving in the area with various adaptions of the *Ordnung* (the unwritten rules the Amish live by,) then who set the standards? I already knew that there were variations in how they dressed, the colors of the buggies, window dressings (mostly green blinds in Pennsylvania), and other distinctions that weren't universal in each community.

I was told that whoever arrived in the area first set the standard for the new district. Then the woman bristled a little as she told me that they were having problems with some of the ladies in the community conforming to the rules. Specifically, some of the women were wearing their dresses too long, and this seemed to be a serious offense.

Before she could elaborate further, her husband came into the room with a stern look on his face and asked his wife if she pointed out my mistake in a book, even cited which page I'd made the error. I had mailed Lydia a copy of my first book in my Daughters of the Promise series, hoping to make her feel more comfortable when I arrived for a visit. At least, she would know that I'd done a lot of research and tried very hard to represent the Amish as authentically as possible. Lydia was introduced to me through a friend of a friend.

My heart pounded against my chest as I apologized for anything they might have found offensive in my book, *Plain Perfect.* The woman spoke barely above a whisper when she said, "We don't smoke. No one smokes. And you have men going out in the barn and smoking cigars after Sunday worship services."

I politely explained to her that in Lancaster County, Pennsylvania, smoking was a common practice following the meal on Sundays. I'd been told this by several people living in and near Paradise, Intercourse, and Bird In

Hand, all Lancaster County towns. Lydia and her husband were shocked.

It would be years later before I decided to write a series in Southern Indiana. There is a place called the Catwalk in Williams, Indiana. It's a popular dam where both Amish and non-Amish folks fish. The Amish man on the next page showed up in a photo I was taking of my husband and friends at the end of the Catwalk.

RUMSCHPRINGE BOYS

Most readers of Amish fiction know that teenagers are allowed a 'running around' period (*rumschpringe*) that begins when they turn sixteen years old. This is an opportunity for the teen to spread his or her wings and experience the outside world prior to choosing baptism. While some parents don't permit their children (*kinner* in Pennsylvania Dutch) to fly far from the nest, most moms and dads look the other way and allow their children freedoms not otherwise considered acceptable.

The thought process, I've been told, is that a child must see how outsiders live in order to choose—or not choose—to be baptized into the faith. Teenagers are not forced into the Amish way of life. If they choose not to be baptized into the faith, they are not shunned by their families. Shunnings only occur if a person has been baptized and refuses to adhere to the *Ordnung* (Amish bylaws that most of the Plain people know by heart).

Surprising to most is the fact that less than five percent of Amish teenagers leave their Amish roots.

During the *rumschpringe*, the young people are allowed to wear English (the word for non-Amish folks) clothes, see movies, listen to music, and cast themselves into a world not yet discovered.

On a normal day in Lancaster County, Pennsylvania, you'll likely see lots of buggies traveling around town in the traditional manner. But during one of my trips to Paradise, a town in Lancaster County, I ran across a group of boys that were definitely enjoying their *rumschpringe*. There were five fellows, and I happened upon them in a parking lot. They were standing outside their buggy, which donned Mardi Gras beads, and loud music boomed from within the buggy. Even though they wore suspenders, their shirts weren't the standard dark colors worn by Amish men. One of the boys had on a pink shirt, and they were all smoking cigarettes. They wore the type of hats the Amish wear, but instead of black loafers or boots, they had on tennis shoes. It was a confusing mish-mash of Amish/English style.

I approached the boys and explained to them that I write Amish fiction and that I was aware they were in their *rumschpringe* (a word that that has a range of spellings within various Amish communities). I boldly asked if I could take their picture. Four out of the five boys agreed to let me take a photograph. One of the teens looked terrified and stood off to the side. I remember thinking at the time that he must come from a conservative family who wouldn't appreciate his new look.

Somewhere I have that picture, which I would never

post in this book or any public forum. It was mostly a slice of research for me. But the visual, which remains in my mind, is filed away in my virtual memory bank to recall upon fondly.

Four boys, dressed in bright colors, their decked out buggy in the background, cigarettes angling from their mouths, shiny new tennis shoes, and boom box music filling the space around them. I haven't seen anything like that again throughout all of my travels in Amish Country.

THE MELTDOWN

There are various versions of this quote, along with different authors who are credited: *There's nothing to writing. All you do is sit down at a typewriter and open a vein.*

In truth, that's how it feels sometimes. But the bleeding turns to hemorrhaging when you manage to turn a large chunk of words into sentences—only to lose it all to a technical glitch, or even worse, user error.

As an author of over forty books, I've had to do plenty of rewrites. Revisions are a necessary, if not tedious, part of the process. Many years ago, I had to rewrite over twenty-thousand words because I thought I was experienced enough to put Jesus on the scene in a book. My editor thought otherwise.

In the year this book is being published, I managed to lose five-thousand words due to 'user error'. Basically, I closed down my computer before the manuscript saved to Dropbox, a software that allows users to log in on any device. It's a handy tool that I've used for a long time. If my computer crashes, I can just go to Hubby's computer, log in to Dropbox, and my manuscript is still there.

But, I was in a hurry, shut down too quickly, then ran 'Clean My Mac' (another techy program to free up space on Mac computers). I rebooted and opened the document, only to learn that NONE of my six hours' worth of beautifully written words were anywhere to be found.

That horrifying event happened at three o'clock in the afternoon. I was still crying and searching when Hubby got home from work at seven. Then I cried and searched for another four hours and didn't get to sleep until after two in the morning.

I personally don't know of any authors who haven't had to endure this type of disaster. It amazes me that I managed to go so long without having to suffer through the experience.

The next morning, I got up and rewrote it all. Some was based on memory, but surprisingly I actually increased my word count from what it was the day before. I write by the seat of my pants, meaning I don't use an outline or plan things out. I figure that if I'm surprised by events, my readers will be too. But, while writing that first draft, I'm also getting to know my characters. It isn't until the next round of writing that I revise scenes based on what I learned while I was getting to know my characters and their motivations. So rewriting that chunk that I'd lost ended up with more depth and layers, which made for a silver lining.

Although, I could do without that type of silver lining in the future.

BONUS SHORT STORY!

An AMISH Adoption

BETH WISEMAN

BESTSELLING AUTHOR

GLOSSARY FOR AN AMISH ADOPTION

Aamen: Amen
boppli: baby
Deitsch: Dutch
Englisch: those who are not Amish; the English language
Gott: God
gut: good
haus: house
kinner: children
lieb: love
mamm: mom
mei: my
nee: no
Ordnung: written and unwritten rules in an Amish district
schweschder: sister
sohn: son
Wie bischt: How are you?
Ya: yes

CHAPTER ONE

Emily stood next to her husband on shaky legs as they peered out their living room window, each with a hand to their forehead, blocking the setting sun.

"He's smaller than I thought he would be." Dylan was cheek to cheek with Emily, the curtain parted barely enough for them to see the Amish woman and boy step out of the black buggy. "Should I go help her tether the horse to the fencepost?"

Emily shook her head. "No, she's done it hundreds of times, I'm sure. She'll be done by the time you get to the street." Dylan quickly put the curtain back in place when Caroline Yoder and Noah Jansen started up the sidewalk.

"I've only seen him twice." Emily bit her lip until it throbbed like her pulse. She and Dylan both stood on the other side of the front door, waiting for the woman and Emily's nephew to knock. "When he was born . . . and at Lauren's funeral."

Dylan put a shaky hand on Emily's back as they looked at each other wide-eyed, when the knock came. In less than a week, Emily had lost her sister and gained a child. She opened the door, forced a smile, and she and Dylan stepped aside so that Caroline and Noah could come in. The woman carried a small red suitcase.

A man from social services had called two days ago and asked if Emily and Dylan would be willing to provide foster care for Lauren's six-year-old son, then possibly adopt him. Emily and Dylan had fostered children before, so they were already registered and in the system. Although, the last time they fostered a child, they both agreed they wouldn't do it anymore. They grew too attached to each little person in their care. It was always a blessing when a child could return to a safe environment with their biological parents, but the emptiness for Emily and Dylan was almost too much to bear, and it often lasted for months. But this was different.

Emily and Dylan introduced themselves to Caroline, an Amish woman who looked to be about Emily's age, maybe mid-thirties. Emily had carefully planned what she would say in an effort to make the transition go as smoothly as possible, but she couldn't seem to find her voice. Even though she'd seen her nephew at the funeral, she'd been so distraught about her sister that she hadn't noticed how much Noah looked like his mother. The boy had Lauren's dark hair and eyes, but most telling was the shape of his mouth. Emily's sister had been blessed with full lips and a gorgeous smile. But Noah wasn't smiling. Emily reminded herself to be strong, not to cry over regrets, but to embrace this opportunity for her and Dylan to finally be parents. It was hard, though, since the tragedy of Lauren's death stayed with Emily like a dark cloud that hovered overhead everywhere she went.

After Dylan closed the door he took the suitcase and set it down. Emily leaned down until she was at eye level with her nephew.

"Hi, Noah." She cleared her throat, aware her voice was shaking. "I'm your Aunt Emily, your mother's sister." Nodding toward her husband, she said, "And that is your Uncle Dylan."

"*Wie bischt*," the boy said softly, his eyes cast downward below the traditional cropped bangs. He wore black slacks held up by suspenders, a blue short-sleeved shirt, and he held his straw hat by his side.

Caroline put a hand on Noah's shoulder. "Remember what we talked about Noah? Use your *Englisch*." The woman waited until Emily stood up and she had both hers and Dylan's attention. "Children speak Pennsylvania *Deitsch* first. They don't start learning *Englisch* until they are five, so Noah tends to bounce back and forth between your language and the *Deitsch* dialect. We've told him to do his best, but to try to speak in *Englisch*."

School had just let out the day before. "We'll have lots of time to get to know each other over the summer."

Noah stared at his black shoes, one with an untied lace. Instinctively, Emily squatted down and began to tie his shoe, but before her hand even reached his foot, Noah stepped backward, turned to Caroline, and lifted his eyes to her. He spoke to her in their native dialect. Emily couldn't understand his words, but the emotion was clear. He didn't want to stay.

Caroline's bottom lip trembled as she blinked her eyes, moist with tears that threatened to spill at any moment. "You are going to be fine, *mei* little man. And I will visit as often as I can." She looked up at Dylan and Emily. "As long as that's okay with your new parents."

New parents. Now, it was Emily who might not be able to hold back her tears. She dabbed at one eye as she nodded.

"Of course. Come visit any time." Dylan pointed over his shoulder to a platter of cookies Emily had laid out on the coffee table. "Noah, do you want a cookie?"

But the child didn't even turn around, only clung to Caroline's black apron.

"We've talked to Noah about this, but it will take some time for him to adjust."

"Don't leave me." Emily's precious nephew threw his tiny arms around Caroline. "Please, please." His cries grew louder, and as a tear slipped down Caroline's cheek, she pulled Noah close.

"*Mei* sweet boy, I will be by to see you very soon." She tried to ease Noah away, but he only held onto Caroline even more, sobbing.

Emily wondered what the relationship was between Caroline and Noah. All she'd been told was that an Amish woman would be delivering Emily's nephew today.

"You must stay with these nice people." Caroline tried again to detach herself from Noah, but he wailed. "You will just have to take him," she said to Dylan.

Emily had a hand over her mouth as she blinked back tears and turned to face her husband. Dylan had a hand on his forehead as he took a deep breath. But he didn't move, his feet seemingly rooted to the floor.

Dylan finally put a hand on the child's back, but Noah screamed even louder.

Stupid, stupid. Why didn't they foresee this? As Lauren's only living relatives—with the exception of Noah's unknown father—Emily had thought Noah would want to live with them. Why didn't she think about him being close to other Amish people?

"Please," Caroline said to Dylan with pleading eyes and tears that streamed down her face.

"How will we reach you?" Emily had lived in Montgomery long enough to know most of the Plain people didn't use a phone. There were exceptions for business purposes and emergencies, but avoiding landlines and mobile devices was the general rule.

"This is *mei* address." Caroline handed Emily a crumpled up piece of paper she had in her hand. Sniffling, she still had a hand on Noah's head and spoke loudly above his cries. "It is always suitable to write to me, but you can be at our *haus* in ten minutes by car."

Emily took the small slip of paper as she swiped away a tear.

Dylan's eyes were moist as he tried to reach for Noah, but he hesitated.

"Please, take him," Caroline said barely above a whisper. Then she forcefully grabbed the boy's arms and held him away from her enough that Dylan was able to wrap his arms around his waist.

Noah kicked and screamed as Dylan carried him

away from the entryway, through the living room, and toward the kitchen.

Caroline wept openly. Emily wanted to hug her, but some of the Amish were funny about affection. Instead, she continued to wipe away her own tears.

She opened her mouth to ask what the relationship was between Caroline and Noah, but Caroline spoke up first.

"Take care of him." Then she spun around, opened the door, and rushed down the sidewalk.

Emily took a couple of steps to follow the woman but stopped. She bent at the waist, put her hands on her knees, and tried to corral her own emotions as Noah continued to wail inside.

Caroline's hands shook as she flicked the reins and set her horse in a steady trot. She would cry all the way home, then put on a happy face for Abraham. At least she'd try to. Her husband was hurting as much as Caroline.

If there was one saving grace in all of this, at least Emily and Dylan lived out in the country. Maybe they raised chickens, or pigs, or had a pet of any kind. Caroline wished she had asked since Noah loves animals.

By the time she got home, Caroline should have been all cried out, but when she saw Abraham standing on the front porch, she exited the buggy, loosely tethered her horse, then ran across the yard. Disregarding all of her predetermined notions, she hurried up the steps and into her husband's arms.

"It was horrible." Caroline grabbed his suspenders as she buried her face against his chest and sobbed. "He screamed and screamed, and finally the *Englisch* man had to pry Noah off of me." She looked up at her husband whose eyes were filled with emotion. "Lauren would have wanted us to have him. She was my best friend, and she didn't have a relationship with her *schweschder*."

"*Ya*, I know." Abraham held her, rubbing her back. "But the law sides with family members."

Caroline stepped back from her husband. "*We* are her family. We've been around Noah since he was born. Lauren's sister showed up at the hospital to see Noah when he arrived, then not again until the funeral. "That's *not* family, Abe." She shook her head, which only caused her temples to throb even more. "If Lauren had been sick, and not died suddenly, she would have made plans for Noah, and she would have wanted for him to be raised here, by us, and grow up in the faith Lauren wanted for him."

Abraham ran his hand the length of his beard, which reached almost to the middle of his chest. They'd been married fourteen years, but God hadn't blessed them with any children. Caroline's stomach cramped up every time she thought about Lauren and the horrible buggy accident that had killed her instantly. But leaving Noah with strangers was shredding her insides.

"We talked to the social worker, and the *Englisch* couple—Noah's aunt and uncle—they haven't been able to have *kinner* either. And they have lots of experience, apparently, since they've taken in and cared for a lot of little ones."

Caroline folded her arms across her chest and looked down. "They don't have experience with Noah. They don't know him." She covered her face, shaking her head. "He's in an unfamiliar world he won't understand."

Abraham wrapped an arm around Caroline and led her into the house. She walked to the counter and eyed the box that she'd forgotten to take to Noah's new parents. It contained his favorite books, the cup he liked, a plastic horse, and a few other toys Caroline had brought from Noah's house. A new couple in the district was already interested in buying the place. Things were moving too quickly for Caroline, and as she put a hand across her stomach, it grumbled. She hadn't eaten today.

Her husband poured a cup of coffee and handed it to her. "Here *mei lieb*."

She took a sip of the hot beverage and set the cup down on the counter. Another tear trickled down her cheek, but there wasn't anything else to be said. Noah would be living with his English aunt and uncle, and there wasn't anything she or Abraham could do about it.

The void in her heart and the emptiness in her womb had never felt heavier. She missed her friend so much it made her physically ill. And when she pictured Noah being pried from her body, screaming, she squeezed her eyes closed and tried to banish the memory. But his cries resounded over and over again, echoing in her mind until she thought she might collapse.

Caroline sat down at the kitchen table and held her head in her hands. Her husband pulled out the chair across from her and eased into it. His tired eyes drooped beneath his bushy eyebrows as he slid his suspenders over his shoulders, then sighed.

"Did you tell the *Englisch* woman about the problems Noah has at night?"

Caroline rubbed her eyes as she shook her head. "*Nee.* I was so upset. And Noah was screaming. I didn't think about it." She nodded to the box on the counter. "I forgot to take his box, and his medicine is in there."

Her husband frowned as he shook his head. "It will be a long night for the new parents."

Caroline hoped so. Maybe they would choose to send Noah back where he belonged.

CHAPTER TWO

Emily hadn't asked what Noah liked to eat or if he was allergic to anything, so she had to assume that he didn't have any known allergies.

"Noah, do you like spaghetti?" Dylan sat across the table from the boy, and Emily held her breath as she stirred the noodles, looking over her shoulder in time to see Noah nod. It had taken over an hour to get him to stop crying after Caroline Yoder left.

"Emily makes the best spaghetti ever." Dylan glanced at Emily and winked at her. He was good with children. They'd had foster kids that weren't easy to manage, but Dylan was patient with all of them. He was a born father, and Emily was excited for them to finally have a chance to be parents. Noah wouldn't be leaving them like the other children they'd cared for. Emily and Dylan would see him graduate, hopefully have a career, and get married someday.

As she looked at Noah right now, you'd have thought he'd lost a dozen best friends. His dark eyes were swollen from crying, and his bottom lip trembled. But he hadn't lost a dozen best friends, only one and she was his mother. He'd been ripped from the only home he'd ever known, and both Dylan and Emily were sensitive to that. They'd fostered children who had been removed from their homes in the middle of the night. Some of those kids had adjusted, and others never did.

Emily put a plate of spaghetti in front of him and sat down. "Dig in," she said.

Noah closed his eyes and lowered his head.

"He's praying," Dylan said, barely above a whisper.

Emily lowered her head but kept one eye open. She and Dylan had tried to encourage a simple prayer before meals with their foster children, but it had slipped their mind this evening. Even though she and Dylan were not particularly religious and didn't attend church, they believed each child should have an opportunity to find his or her way when it came to a higher entity. Prayer before meals was their way of an introduction in that regard. God wasn't something Emily and Dylan talked about, but she should have known Noah would be religious. They were going to raise him as their son so that made the spiritual aspect a bit complicated, but she wanted to respect what Noah had been taught so far.

Sometimes Emily felt a presence, a voice in her head, something coaxing her to explore the possibility of a relationship with God. Whatever pull she felt also seemed out of reach. Not wanting to leave any stone unturned, she had prayed for God to bless them with a child of their own. The blessing had come with a price though.

Surprisingly, her nephew—soon to be son—ate all of his spaghetti, and afterward, bath time went smoothly as well. By the time she tucked Noah into bed, his eyelids were heavy. Since Emily and Dylan had fostered children before, one of their spare bedrooms was decorated for a child Noah's age. She'd kept the colors neutral for a boy or girl—and they'd had both over the years—and it was a cheerful room. The double bed was covered in a yellow comforter with teddy bears riding bicycles. There were stars on the ceiling that glowed at night. There was a toy box filled with various items that were safe for children three years old and older. Down the hallway, they had another bedroom that was more suited to preteens and teenagers, and they'd cared for a few children that age as well.

"Do you want me to read you a story?" Emily fought the yawn working its way up from her throat, but story time had helped her to bond with some of the other young children they'd kept.

Noah shook his head. Emily wanted to kiss him on the forehead or cup his cheek and tell him everything was going to be okay, but anything she said would be hollow words to him right now.

"Dylan and I are just next door in our bedroom. So, if you need anything, come and get us, okay?" It was way too soon for them to suggest he call them mommy and daddy, but just the thought of she and Dylan as parents caused her heart to swell. Although the emotion was tempered again by the price that had been paid for Emily and Dylan to have a child. Her sister's life. Emily cringed as she recalled the harsh words she and Lauren had the last time they talked to each other. She took a deep breath and forced the memories aside.

She placed a blue teddy bear in bed next to Noah and left a nightlight on in the corner. There was also a glass of water on the nightstand. When he yawned, Emily did too.

"How do you feel about pancakes in the morning?" Emily smiled, hoping to entice the tiniest bit of positive emotion from Noah, but he just nodded and maintained the blank look he'd had most of the evening.

"Sleep tight." She backed out of the room and blew him a kiss before she crossed the threshold.

"Did you leave the door open?" Dylan was atop the covers reading when Emily walked into their bedroom. He lowered the book to his lap. In the past, they'd taken turns tucking in young children, giving them some bonding time with each child. They'd been good foster parents. Emily hoped they would be even better parents.

"Yeah, I left it open, and the nightlight is on. He knows where the bathroom is, so I think he'll be okay for tonight." She slipped out of her robe and got into bed with her husband. "You can tell the poor kid is exhausted."

"It's been a long day." He reached over and found her hand, gave it a squeeze. "I can tell you're worn out too."

She fluffed her pillow, but instead of lying back, she scooted over and cuddled next to Dylan, finding the comfy nook between his neck and shoulder. There had been so much to do today that she hadn't allowed herself to think about Lauren. When memories had forged to the front of her mind, she'd forced them away. But now, all was quiet, and it was all she could think about. She was plagued with regret.

"Thinking about Lauren?" Dylan pulled her closer.

"Yeah." She heard the shakiness in her voice. "All these years, she's lived less than fifteen minutes from us, and I never visited her, or went to see Noah." She paused as her chest tightened. "We said awful things to each other the last time we spoke."

"Don't do that to yourself, Em. Lauren forbade you to come see her or Noah, and she never came to visit us."

"I should have tried harder, but I never forgave her for not coming home when mom died. Our mother had raised us by herself for most of our lives. Daddy was only twenty-four when he died. Lauren should have been at the funeral."

"Try not to look back." Dylan kissed her on the forehead. "Instead, we'll put our efforts into being the best parents we can."

As she looked up at Dylan, she thought about how lucky she was to be his wife. Her husband wasn't just handsome and kind, he was compassionate and genuine. "Have you noticed how everyone in my family dies young? My dad. And, then my mom was only fifty-one when she passed. And my sister was twenty-eight." She rolled onto her back. "Maybe I'll go young too."

"Don't say that."

She looked at Dylan. He didn't use that stern voice very often. "Sorry."

"And, you said yourself that when your mom died, Lauren was all messed up, doing drugs, running with the wrong people, and jobless most of the time."

"Yeah, she was, and I'm glad she got straightened out but did it have to be with the Amish? I mean, couldn't she have found another religion to help put her life back together again? The way the Amish choose to stay apart from everyone didn't help Lauren and me to mend our relationship. If anything, the Amish ways discouraged it."

"I don't know, but there's nothing you can do about any of it. All we can focus on is being good parents to Noah."

Emily turned onto her side, gazed into her husband's eyes, and smiled. "Do you know how much I love you?"

"I should. You've told me hundreds of times." He rolled his eyes before he turned on his side facing her. "I believe it's to the moon and back times infinity."

"Correct," she whispered before a tear slipped down her cheek. Dylan brushed it away with his thumb and ran a hand through her shoulder-length blonde hair.

"I know you loved Lauren, and she loved you. Over time, I think you would have worked things out."

"I don't know. I could have tried harder to have a relationship with her," she repeated. "But I could only take so many rejections, and . . ." She began to cry, really cry hard for the first time since her sister had died. "She'll never see her son grow up."

Dylan pulled her into his arms and held her. He let her lie there and cry, knowing that was what she needed right now.

Exhaustion and grief met up, and Emily dozed off in her husband's arms. She didn't know how long she'd been sleeping when she awoke to a loud voice. It wasn't a scream. It was just loud talking. She jabbed Dylan with her elbow.

"Wake up." She got out of bed and threw on her robe as she ran around the corner to Noah's room. "Noah!" She rushed into his empty bedroom before heading down the hallway, realizing the loud voice was coming from the living room.

Emily's nephew didn't turn around when she said his name several times. Two at a time, Noah pulled books from the shelf on one side of the television and tossed them on the floor. He spoke in the language he was most familiar with, and his voice was loud. Emily wasn't sure what to do.

"He's sleepwalking," Dylan whispered as he came up beside her. "Don't wake him up. We just need to guide him back to his room. Remember, like we did with Brian?"

Emily nodded. They'd only had one foster child who walked in his sleep, but there hadn't been any yelling or throwing things.

When Dylan approached Noah, he put a hand on his arm. "Let's go back to bed, Buddy." He tried to gently nudge the child, but Noah wiggled loose and went toward the kitchen. Emily and Dylan rushed after him. He went from drawer to drawer, opening and slamming each one. Emily had child-proofed the house years ago. There weren't any sharp objects in the drawers. Knives were kept up high in a cabinet.

"Noah, Sweetie. Let's go to bed." Emily reached for him, but he cried out, again speaking a language Emily didn't understand." She glanced at Dylan. When their sleepwalker—Brian—had walked in his sleep, they were able to gently guide him back to bed, then go back to sleep themselves. Brian was ten when they fostered him for about three months. But he'd never had this type of outburst.

"Do you think this is normal?" Emily whispered to Dylan after Noah stopped opening drawers and began circling the kitchen table. "Or maybe it's because of the move, his mother. . ." She didn't even want to say the word, but 'died' would be forever associated with the mention of Noah's mother or in reference to Emily's sister.

Dylan shrugged but moved toward Noah. "Hey, Buddy. Let's go back to bed." He tried to latch onto Noah's hand, but he jerked away, then leaned against the kitchen wall so hard that the dishes in the nearby china cabinet rattled.

Emily held her breath as Noah's eyes widened. "Caroline?" He screamed the woman's name.

"He's awake," Dylan said in a whisper before he slowly moved toward the frightened six-year-old. He crouched down in front of him. "You're okay, Noah. Remember Caroline brought you to stay with us? You're safe here. Maybe you had a bad dream?"

Noah's eyes were still opened wide, but he had stopped talking loudly and moving around. Emily was tempted to reach for the cookie jar, but she hated to give him sugar at two in the morning.

After a minute or so, Noah yawned, and he let Dylan pick him up. Noah even rested his head on Dylan's shoulder.

Emily followed them to Noah's bedroom. Dylan carefully laid him in the bed, and Emily pulled up the cover, then kissed him on the forehead.

After they tiptoed back to their bedroom, Emily said, "I wonder if he's ever done that before."

Dylan eased back into bed, yawning. "I don't know. Some kids sleepwalk, and most of them grow out of it."

"But I don't think most of them throw books, open doors, and run around the house." She paused as she got comfortable beside her husband again. "Did you see the look on his face when he woke up? He looked terrified."

"I got up once with Brian when he was sleepwalking, and he woke up. He looked scared, too, at first." Dylan got prone and moved closer to Emily until he had an arm draped across her.

She wondered how often her husband thought about ten-year-old Brian. Emily still thought about him all the time, even more than the other children they'd cared for. Brian had been raised by his grandmother since his parents were in jail for dealing drugs. The judge hadn't gone lightly on them. Even though Brian's grandmother was granted custody of the child, Emily always wondered if he had returned to a safe place and a loving environment. Ties were severed between foster children and their temporary parents. The social workers said it was for the best. Emily wasn't sure about that. She reminded herself that this was different, that she and Dylan would file the papers to start the adoption process. They wouldn't have to return Noah to anyone or ever worry if he was being properly cared for.

"We will be good parents to Noah," she said through

a yawn. "I might not have been a good sister, but I will be a good mother to Lauren's son."

Dylan sighed. "Stop blaming yourself. Lauren is the one who chose to stay detached from anyone who isn't Amish," her husband reminded her again. "That's the way they live. They keep to themselves."

It was a conversation they'd had many times. Emily's youngest sister was living a life Emily and her mother didn't approve of before becoming involved with the Amish. After her mother died, Emily recalled Lauren telling her she was pregnant. Emily was angry with Lauren for not coming home in time for their mother's funeral. She'd been somewhere in Oklahoma at the time with one of her many boyfriends. But, equally as upsetting, was the fact that Lauren was pregnant.

Emily and Dylan had been trying for six years to have a child of their own with no luck. She squeezed her eyes closed as she recalled the terrible fight with her sister.

She'd heard through the grapevine, which was small in Montgomery, Indiana, that Emily had shacked up with the Amish. She probably didn't have anywhere else to go since Emily refused to let her live with her and Dylan. And now she was gone.

CHAPTER THREE

Dylan was flipping pancakes as Emily set the table when there was a knock at the door around nine the following morning. She glanced at Noah seated at the table drinking orange juice.

"Be right back." She shuffled in her socks and robe to the front door, wondering who would be visiting so early on a Saturday. Friends and neighbors had inquired about meeting Noah, but they'd gently asked everyone to give them time alone for a short while. That way Noah could adjust to them as a family of three first.

She opened the door and startled. "Caroline."

The Amish woman held up a brown paper bag, and she held a box in the other. Lifting the bag, she said, "I forgot to give this to you yesterday." Her eyes were still swollen as if she'd had the same emotional night as Emily. "Sometimes Noah walks in his sleep, and this herbal remedy helps him." She lifted the box. "And these are a few of his favorite things."

Emily nodded as she took the bag and the box. "Yes,

we had quite a night. We've had sleepwalkers in our care before, but nothing like last night."

"I'm sorry." Caroline lowered her head, and it was impossible not to feel sorry for the woman. "I should have told you." She looked around Emily, who stood just inside the door. "Is Noah all right? I thought maybe I could just tell him hello."

Emily stepped over the threshold and pulled the door closed behind her. She took a deep breath. "Caroline, I can tell you care a great deal for Noah. But I'm not sure that seeing him right now is a good idea. I'm afraid we'll have another scene like yesterday. And, right now, we're trying to make him feel safe and loved. I know we said to visit anytime, but maybe we can hold off on a visit for now, until Noah gets used to us."

Caroline lowered her head again but nodded before she looked up at Emily. "Of course. You're right. He's just been such a huge part of our lives since he was born, mine and Abraham's, *mei* husband."

Emily could feel the emotion radiating from this Amish woman she didn't know. "Can I ask how it is that you are so close to Noah?"

Caroline reached for a tissue in her apron pocket, then dabbed at her eyes. "Lauren was *mei* best friend. When she showed up in our community, she was quite a mess. Homeless, pregnant, and lost. The Troyers found her sleeping in their barn. We had the most room at our house since we don't have any children." She paused to clear her throat. "We took her in and tended to her while she was pregnant. She lived with us until Noah was born, then they both were with us until

Lauren was able to get a job and a place of her own a few months later. I kept Noah during the days when Lauren worked." A slight smile lifted her expression. "We were so proud of her. She said she'd been at the bottom, but we were blessed to watch her rise to the top. It wasn't long before she chose to be baptized into our faith. She never married, but she was a *gut mudder* to Noah."

Emily could feel her emotions bubbling to the surface, swirling together in a tornado of confusion. Regrets suffocated her, and she was tempted to let Caroline come in and see Noah, to relieve some of the pain the woman was feeling. But, as Noah's mother now, she wanted to do what was best for him. Emily also wanted to know more about Lauren, but that would need to come later too.

"There are a lot of things I'd like to know about my sister." Emily looked past Caroline as her thoughts continued to skew and collide. "And I know this is an extremely difficult situation for Noah . . ." She paused, rubbing her forehead. "I just think that we need this time, just Noah, my husband, and me, to establish a solid foundation for Noah. We know how big of a change this is for him, and how hard it must be for you." Emily swallowed hard. "We want Noah to have a relationship with you and your husband, but we want him to recognize that we will be his parents."

Caroline nodded, her eyes cast down for a few moments before she looked at Emily. "*Ya*, I understand. I just . . ." She blotted her eyes. "I just don't want him to forget us." After shrugging, she let the tears flow. "Or maybe he should forget us. Maybe that would be best for Noah."

Emily's chest was tight as she blinked back tears. "I won't let that happen." She made the statement with a conviction she planned to honor. She recalled how she felt every time one of their foster children had left. "I promise," she said barely above a whisper.

Caroline nodded, then turned to leave.

Emily watched her walk down the sidewalk to her horse and buggy as she tried to envision her sister living that type of life.

After she went back into the house, she dried her eyes and started back to the kitchen, but went into her bedroom instead. As much as she'd like to give Noah the box with his favorite things, he would know it had been Caroline at the door. She could pass off the medication like she'd forgotten to give it to him last night.

Dylan was flipping the pancakes high in the air and failing miserably when she entered the kitchen. As one of the flapjacks landed in the sink, Noah laughed, and it was more than just music to Emily's ears, it was the sound of family. There had been a lot of laughter in the room over the years, and she and Dylan had been grateful for the opportunity to provide relief for children in need. But they'd always known it was temporary. This wasn't, and it felt wonderfully different.

Noah sat at a chair at the table, his expression bright. Emily touched him on the shoulder as she made her way to her husband. "He isn't a very good pancake flipper, is he?"

The child shook his head, grinning. "*Nee*, not *gut* at all."

"Hey, now." Dylan flipped another pancake, this time catching it in the pan. "If you two want to eat, be nice to the cook." He glanced at Emily. "Who was at the door?"

She held up the bag before placing it on the counter. "A delivery. I'll explain later."

Noah giggled when Dylan missed the mark again, this time the pancake landed on the floor.

Emily sat down beside Noah. "Yuck, I'm not eating that one. Are you?"

Noah shook his head, and Emily thought her heart might burst with happiness as he held onto the smile. But she wasn't a hundred percent in the moment. Noah looked so much like Lauren that it was hard to push thoughts of her sister aside.

After the salvaged pancakes were on a plate in the middle of the table, next to a platter of bacon and bowl of scrambled eggs, Noah bowed his head.

Emily glanced at Dylan and they lowered their heads as well. Even though they'd often said prayers aloud with children in their care before, Emily found herself wondering what Noah was praying about. Was he thanking God for the food? Did he want God to send him back to Caroline's house?

She decided not to speculate, but to offer up her own prayers, which felt awkward since she hadn't ever prayed on a regular basis. But she'd never been in a role as crucial as this one. It wasn't a temporary situation. She would forever be a mother to Noah.

Dear God, I'm unworthy of the gift of this child You've

sent to us, but I pray that Dylan and I will be the best parents we can be and that we will always make the best decisions for Noah. She paused when she thought she felt something deep inside, a feeling she didn't recognize, a type of warmth, an understanding. Was it God? Did He actually hear her? She'd had similar feelings before but was never sure. She lifted her head and locked eyes with Dylan, who smiled. Noah continued to pray.

When he finally looked up, Dylan said, "Let's eat!"

Emily helped Noah spread butter on his pancakes, and their new family member reached for two pieces of bacon. After they filled their plates and everyone was eating, Emily had one more prayer to silently say. *Thank you, God.*

Caroline fought tears all the way home, despite the sunshine and colorful foliage on either side of the road. The warm temperature of early summer mixed with the hint of a leftover spring breeze. There wasn't a cloud in the sky, but the clouds across Caroline's heart weren't going to lift any time soon.

Emily and her husband seemed like nice people. Caroline knew that Lauren's relationship with her sister hadn't been good, and she was certain Lauren would have wanted Noah with her and Abraham, but the Lord's will was being done, and Caroline needed to accept it. If only her heart could get in sync with the logic of it all.

Abraham was washing his hands under the pump near the gate when Caroline pulled in. Sniffling, she did her best to wipe away her tears. Her husband was hurting, too, and seeing her cry would only make things worse for him.

He wiped his hands on his shirt and searched her eyes. "How was Noah?"

Caroline raised her chin and stood taller. "I didn't get to see him. Emily thought it would be best for Noah if they establish themselves as a family before he sees us." Despite all her efforts, her bottom lip began to quiver. "She's probably right," she said in a whisper, longing for comfort from her husband. Instead, his face turned red.

"Nothing is right about this situation. Noah should be with us." He turned away from her, and Caroline suspected it was to hide his feelings. She walked up behind him and put her arms around him, resting her head against his back.

"I might be wrong, Abe, but I think Emily and her husband will allow us to have a place in Noah's life." She squeezed her eyes closed as she kept her head pressed against her husband.

"His place should be here." He slowly turned around, his eyes red with emotion. "We don't even know if they are people of faith. Noah won't know the teachings of the *Ordnung*. Do they even go to church?"

Caroline cupped her husband's cheek as his eyes watered, along with her own. "We've talked about all of this, Abe. We have to trust the Lord's will." In reality, Caroline wanted to lash out at God, to scream, to go back and snatch Noah from the English. But she chose, instead, to offer comfort to her husband.

Abraham reached for her hand, then pressed it to his lips, kissing it tenderly. "I know."

They walked hand in hand across the front yard, up the porch steps, and into their quiet house. A place of great sorrow following Lauren's death. But then, there had been laughter as they'd tried to brighten Noah's days.

Now, it was just quiet.

"What's in the bag?" Dylan asked in a whisper as they cleared the breakfast dishes. Noah had gone to his bedroom, which Emily had stocked with everything a six-year-old might like.

"It was Caroline at the door, and she said it's herbs that helped Noah sleep without having nightmares." She sighed as she placed two plates in the dishwasher. "I feel sorry for her."

Dylan opened the small paper bag. "It looks like candy, round chocolate candy." He raised an eyebrow as he took one out and inspected it. "Are the herbs supposed to be inside? How do we know it's safe?"

Emily placed their forks in the dishwasher tray, then stood up and wiped her hands on a kitchen towel. "They love Noah. I don't think they'd do anything to harm him. They sent over a box with some of his favorite things, but I'll give that to him when he's better settled. He'd know Caroline was here."

"There's only six in the bag." Dylan dropped the round chocolate ball back into the bag.

"I guess that's her excuse to come back over, or for us

to go to her for more, assuming it works." Emily recalled the sorrow etched across Caroline's face. "She wanted to see Noah, but I explained to her that we needed to establish ourselves as a family. I told her I worried we'd have another scene like before. I could tell she was disappointed, but she seemed to understand and want what's best for Noah."

"Six more days isn't enough time to establish a family unit." Dylan set the bag back on the counter. "I'll take one tonight before bed. I don't want to give Noah anything without trying it first."

"That might mean another night of sleepwalking, but I agree that one of us should probably try it first." She smiled a little. "And you're the one who has the most trouble falling asleep. Maybe Caroline will give us some extras for you if it works."

"Seems weird to give a kid chocolate right before bed." Dylan frowned. "I guess we give it to him, then he can brush his teeth. But I'll try one first."

"Should we go check on him?" Emily asked before they'd even finished cleaning the kitchen. "There are tons of toys in his room, but have you noticed that when I turn on the TV, he walks away? I figured he would be thrilled to have a television since the Amish don't allow it."

"Maybe he thinks he's breaking the rules if he watches it, even though we told him it was okay." Dylan motioned with his hand. "Let's go take a peek at him."

Emily followed her husband to their son's bedroom, tiptoeing in their socks until they were in the doorway. Emily brought a hand to her chest and bit her bottom lip. Noah had lifted the window and had his face pressed up against the screen. Two horses and buggies were going down the road. He'd arrived with his straw hat, and he had left it in his room. But he wore it now.

"Noah?" Dylan spoke softly. It took a few seconds for the child to turn around, and Emily's breath seized in her throat when he did. Tears rolled down his sweet face which was streaked red.

"I want to go home," he said, barely able to catch his breath.

Emily wanted to tell him that he was home, that he had two parents who would love him until the end of time. She slowly shuffled toward him and bent down. "Honey, everything is going to be okay," she whispered as she put a hand on his arm. He didn't jerk away from her, but he wouldn't look at her either.

"I want to go home," he said again, still struggling to catch his breath.

Emily glanced over her shoulder at Dylan still standing in the doorway, his face looking drawn, his expression one of pained confusion.

Finally, Noah turned to Emily. "*Mei* visit is over. I want to be home with *men mamm*."

Emily put her free hand on her stomach, right were the punch to the gut might as well have happened. "Sweetie, I know Caroline talked to you about your mommy, that she went to be with God. Right?"

Dylan walked to the other side of Noah and touched his head. "It makes us so happy to have you here," he said, trying to sound upbeat. "Do you think maybe you could stay a while longer? I know you miss your mom, but I think if you give it—"

"I want Caroline and Abraham!" This time Noah screamed so loud that Emily and Dylan both flinched before they locked eyes. They'd both been trained and experienced situations like this, but it hadn't hit so close to home before. This child was Emily's flesh and blood, her nephew at the very least. But as she stared at this terrified, screaming, unhappy child, Emily saw her sister.

She lowered her head and covered her face, knowing she wasn't handling things correctly at all. But it felt like someone was clawing at her insides, unearthing feelings she'd tried to avoid. She couldn't stop crying as she fell from her squatting position all the way to the floor.

"Hey, Buddy, why don't we go outside and watch for more buggies?" Dylan's voice was shaky, but Noah sucked in air, his cries becoming more of a whimper. "We have a lot of buggies go by on the dirt road."

Noah let Dylan pick him up. "Let's give Emily a few minutes to herself."

She was glad Dylan hadn't referred to her as mommy, a title she hadn't earned yet.

As she watched from the window, her husband carried Noah into the front yard and they sat down facing the street together.

Emily pulled her knees to her chest and wrapped her arms around herself, tears spilling onto her white robe. As upset as she was about Noah, there was an underlying pain so acute, she wondered if she was going to throw up.

I'm so sorry, Lauren. I'm sorry I didn't make more of an effort to help you, to get to know you in your new life, to have an opportunity while you were alive to love your son, to see you as a mommy . . . I'm sorry.

CHAPTER FOUR

Emily bolted straight up when she heard movement coming from Noah's bedroom. It sounded like he was opening and closing his dresser drawer. She nudged Dylan, who had fallen directly asleep after popping one of the chocolate balls in his mouth. Emily thought the herbs were supposed to stop sleepwalking, not sedate a person.

"Dylan!"

Emily didn't wait for her husband and rushed from her bedroom to Noah's, where he was indeed slamming the middle drawer of his dresser repeatedly.

She touched him on the arm. "Let's go back to bed, Noah," she whispered in the darkness. Only the light of the moon shone into the room, along with a nightlight in the corner.

When he kept slamming the drawers, she wondered how Dylan was sleeping through this. "Honey, let's don't do that," she said as she gently took hold of one of Noah's wrists. He jerked away, screamed, and ran into the wall, knocking himself down.

"Noah!"

Emily darted toward the light switch, flipped it on, then ran and picked him up. She could already see a goose egg forming on his forehead. As he began to flail and wiggle, she was about to drop him so she set him down. He backed away from her until he was up against the dresser.

"You're not *Mamm*! You're not *Mamm*!" he cried.

"No, baby, I'm not." Emily fought to keep from crying. Noah was awake and confused. "But I'm going to help you get tucked into bed, okay?"

He darted across the room to the far corner, like an animal being trapped, his eyes wild and searching hers.

"Noah, you're okay. Nothing is going to hurt you. You were dreaming, and now it's time to get back in bed." *Dylan, where are you?*

"I want Caroline." He flattened his palms against the walls on either side of him. "*Mamm* said you should let me live with Caroline."

Emily covered her face with her hands, but quickly lowered her arms. This wasn't a time to fall apart. She eased closer to Noah, and when he lowered his arms, relaxing a little, she walked all the way to him and once again scrunched down.

"You must have been dreaming about your mother. I bet that was nice, seeing her in your dreams." Emily wished she could see her sister in her dreams. Sometimes she saw her mother and others who had passed, but not Lauren. She reached up to touch Noah's forehead, to at least turn his head to have a better look at the growing knot, but he moved to the side and out of her reach. "I think we need to put some ice on your head. Can you come with me to the kitchen?" She forced a smile. "And I think maybe some cookies and milk are in order. What do you think?"

He stopped crying but merely stared at her. "*Mamm* said you should let me live with Caroline," he said again.

Emily lowered her head, planned out what she would say, then looked back at the tearful child in front of her. "I know you think that's what mommy said, but the best place for you to be is here. I'm your mother's sister. We grew up together, and . . ." Emily started to recall the ways she'd failed her younger sister, but she cleared her throat, determined to keep herself together.

"She also said she forgives you," Noah said softly.

Emily tensed. "What?"

"*Mamm* said she forgives you. And she said she wants you to forgive her." Noah's gaze met hers as a tear trickled down Emily's cheek.

With slow intent, Noah reached up and brushed away Emily's tear. She didn't move, just stared at this gorgeous boy her sister had been gifted, only for them to be parted much too soon.

It was unexpected when Noah wrapped his arms around Emily's neck, but it was such a gratifying gesture that Emily couldn't hold back her tears.

"Don't cry," Noah said softly as he patted her on the back.

"God, if you are there, I need some clarity," she said as she cried in Noah's arms. It was a role reversal and in the worst possible way. A six-year-old who'd recently lost his mother, and everything he'd ever known, was comforting her.

Noah leaned away from her and put a hand to his chest. "*Gott* is always right here. *Mamm* said that. Caroline says that too." His eyes watered up again. "Can I please go see Caroline and Abraham tomorrow?"

Emily stared at the beautiful child in front of her and nodded. "But only if you let me put some ice on your forehead and eat cookies with me."

Noah smiled. "*Ya*, okay."

The next morning Emily awoke early, her eyes swollen and sore. She rolled on to her side, and Dylan smiled. "Best night's sleep I've had in a long time." Then he noticed her eyes. "What's wrong?"

"Well, I'm not sure we should ever give those little chocolate balls to Noah. It was like you took a sleeping pill." After yawning, Emily filled him in on everything that happened. Somehow she managed to do it without crying.

"Em, it had to have been truly emotional for you, but do you think you should have agreed to take him to see Caroline and her husband? We were going to wait on that, get him stable here first, feeling like he belonged in our family."

She squeezed her eyes closed and sighed. "I know, I know, but I kept seeing Lauren's face blending with

Noah's, and there was such great sadness. I just wanted to make him happy."

"You can't break your promise." He ran a hand through his hair. "I've got a lot to do today, even though it's Sunday, but I can hold off on some of it and go with you if you want."

Dylan was an architect with more clients than he could handle sometimes. He worked from home, which often meant seven days per week in some capacity.

"No, no. I'll go. If it's a setback, we'll have to deal with it." She yawned again. "They have church every other Sunday so they might not be home." She had mixed feelings about whether to hope for that. "But I want to talk to Caroline about Lauren too. It seems like I have a lot of unresolved feelings bubbling to the surface, and I guess I want to know more about my sister's life."

Dylan leaned closer and kissed her on the forehead before he pulled her into the nook of his arm, the place she felt safest. "You know, we are going to get through all this. We are going to be wonderful parents and give Noah a good life. It might be different than what he's used to. There will be more tears, I'm sure. But, between the two of us, we have enough love to give that child to last a lifetime." They were quiet for a while. "I know you've always had some unresolved issues about Lauren, but you never wanted to talk much about it. But, Em, she was a grownup making her own decisions."

"But I was her older sister. I knew where she lived. I even knew she had a son." She buried her head against Dylan's chest. "I should have reached out to her."

He eased her away. "You *did.* And she didn't want anything to do with you."

"But she didn't want me in her life because I was so critical of the way she was living. She was wild when she first left home, then when she went to live with the Amish, I called them a cult and said awful things to her." A tear rolled down her cheek. "And now I can't tell her how sorry I am."

He kissed her forehead. "It sounds like maybe she knows."

Emily lifted her head and stared at her husband. They rarely talked about God, just enough to be good foster parents, encouraging the children to pray and be grateful. "Do you believe in God, Dylan? I mean, do you *truly* believe? Do you think there's even the slightest possibility that what Noah said could be true?"

He was quiet and still for several long moments. "Yeah, I believe."

"Then why don't we ever talk about it?" She scooted back a little and propped herself up on her elbow. "Do you pray?"

"Yes."

Wow. There was no hesitation at all.

"Do you?" he asked.

She pressed her lips together. "Probably not as much as I should. Mostly when I need something." She cringed, but then remembered giving thanks for Noah recently.

They both jumped and separated when there was a knock at the door.

"Come in," Dylan said.

Noah walked in dressed in the clothes he had arrived

in—black slacks, a short-sleeved dark blue shirt, and he was wearing his suspenders and hat.

"Can we go see Caroline and Abraham now?"

Emily smiled. She couldn't help it. Noah's excitement about the trip spread from ear to ear. "Yes, but let's eat some breakfast first, okay?"

He nodded and skipped off toward the kitchen.

"This is probably a mistake," she said after he was out of earshot, "but he'll never trust me if I don't keep my promise."

As Emily rolled out of bed, a list of questions swam through her mind, things she wanted to ask Caroline about Lauren. Then she thought about how awful it was going to be dragging Noah back home, probably kicking and screaming.

"Just some eggs and bacon?" she asked as she slipped into her robe.

Dylan nodded.

Emily yawned all the way to the kitchen. Noah was already seated at the table, and Dylan joined them shortly.

Once everything was on the table, Noah lowered his head, and Emily and Dylan followed suit. Emily cleared her throat. "Noah?"

He looked up, and so did Dylan. "Noah, I know that you've always said your prayers quietly to yourself, but I was wondering if maybe you would like to say them out loud? It's our tradition to say prayers together, to thank God for our food and blessings." Emily felt the sting of the tiny lie since they actually only prayed aloud when they were fostering children.

Noah tipped his head to one said. "You mean say the words in my mind out loud?"

"If that's okay with you? Or maybe we can each say a prayer out loud. Do you want me to go first?"

There was a twinkle in Dylan's eyes before he winked at her, then Noah nodded.

Emily wanted to thank God for Noah, but sharing that aloud wouldn't be in Noah's best interest.

She rubbed her nose, shifted her weight in the chair, and finally said, "Um . . . dear Lord, we thank you for our food, for giving us a roof over our heads, and, uh . . . for loving us." She looked across the table at Dylan. "Do you want to go next?"

"Sure." He bowed his head and reached out his arms to hold Emily and Dylan's hands, something she couldn't recall him doing before, even when fostering. This truly was a family now, *their* family. "God, we thank you for the gift of family, for this food as the nourishment for our bodies, and for the many blessings you've bestowed on us. We pray for continued blessings for all those we love. Amen."

Emily smiled at her husband before she turned to Noah. The small boy lowered his head and closed his eyes. "Dear *Gott*, if you can't send back *mei mamm*, please let *mei* live with Caroline and Abraham. *Aamen*."

Noah looked up and reached for a slice of bacon as if he hadn't just gutted Emily with his words. Dylan lowered his head. Emily knew there would be times like this, she just didn't know how much it would hurt. But it would take time for Noah to feel like they were a real family.

Not much was said during the meal, and when Emily asked Noah if he wanted to watch television, he shook his head and went to his bedroom.

"I know he's going to throw a fit when it comes time to leave Caroline and Abraham's." Emily tightened the belt on her robe as she sighed.

Dylan had already started to clean the kitchen. "I got this, the dishes. But, I can go with you if you need me—"

"No." She tucked her hair behind her ears. "It's okay." She took a few steps toward the bedroom before she looked over her shoulder. "I might wish you'd have gone with me when the kicking and screaming starts at the end of our visit."

Dylan kept his head down as he loaded the dishwasher.

"Thanks for cleaning up," she said before she rounded the corner.

About forty-five minutes later, Emily and Noah were ready to leave, and Dylan was in his office laying out sketches of his current project .

"Okay, well, we're off," she said as she peeked inside the room, Noah by her side.

"Okay. Have fun, Noah. See you in a little while."

They both waited for a response, but Noah just scooted quickly toward the front door.

Caroline collected eggs, the way she did every morning, but now Noah wasn't by her side helping. He loved the chickens, even their ornery rooster who seemed to only tolerate Noah, and not anyone else.

She didn't look up when she heard a car turning on their road until the blue minivan pulled into their driveway. After she scooped up two more eggs, she closed the gate on the chicken coop and trudged across the front yard. She wasn't expecting anyone this morning, certainly no one English on a Sunday morning. Then a familiar little person emerged from the passenger door and sprinted toward her.

She set the basket down and held her arms wide as she ran toward him, swallowing him up in a giant bear hug and smothering him with kisses. "I'm so happy to see you!" Squeezing him tighter, she looked over his shoulder at Emily as the woman closed the car door and moved toward her. Her elation foundered as she wondered what was wrong. She eased Noah away, kissed him on the cheek, and noticed the bump on his forehead.

"Why don't you run into the *haus* and see Abraham. He's painting the mudroom."

Noah darted toward the farmhouse as Caroline folded her arms across her chest. "What happened to Noah's head?" Even though she'd tried not to sound accusatory, she heard the implication in her voice.

"He had another episode with sleepwalking. But he woke up and got startled, hitting his head on the wall." The woman was dressed in a colorful sundress filled with floral blooms, and her nails and lipstick matched the rose-colored pattern perfectly. It was hard to picture Noah living with her.

"Did you give him one of the chocolate balls?" Caroline scowled, knowing her voice probably reflected her attitude. "Without them, he won't sleep and will almost always get up during the night."

"I didn't want to give him anything we hadn't tested ourselves since it isn't something prescribed by a doctor." Emily's tone seemed to confirm that she'd taken the comments as a jab. "My husband took one, and it was as if he'd taken sleeping pills."

Caroline didn't want to owe this woman any explanations, but she took a deep breath and reminded herself that seeing Noah was at Emily's discretion. "Noah used to take a lesser amount of herbs inside, just enough to control the sleepwalking. But after Lauren died, the child was exhausted, but he couldn't go to sleep. I should have told you that. Hopefully, he won't need as strong a dose after a while, but I assure you they are safe. I will give you a list of ingredients and you can check with your *Englisch* doctor if you'd like."

Emily nodded, then pushed a pair of pink sunglasses up on her head. "Can we sit somewhere and talk?"

Caroline wished she'd leave so they could spend time with Noah, but she motioned to the two rocking chairs on the porch. After they both sat down, Caroline said, "I'm surprised you brought him to see us. When I stopped by yesterday, you didn't think it was a *gut* idea."

"I still don't." Emily leaned her head back against the high-backed wooden rocker and sighed. "But it was the only way I could get him to calm down during his episode, and I also wanted to talk to you."

Despite it all, Caroline wanted the transition to be

the easiest it could be for Noah. "I'm happy to answer any questions you have about Noah."

Emily twisted in the chair to face Caroline. "Actually, I would like to talk to you about Lauren."

"What about?" Alarms went off for Caroline. She didn't want to betray her friend.

"Last night, after Noah woke up during his sleep-walking, he said he saw his mother in his dreams." She waited, as if for confirmation.

"And you don't believe him?" Noah had often said he saw his mother in his dreams. Caroline had mixed feelings about whether or not such things happened, or if Noah just wished it to be so.

She rubbed her temples. "I don't know what to believe, but he said something that I'm hoping you can explain." She lowered her hands to her lap. "He said that Lauren forgives me and that she wants me to forgive her too." Pausing, she rubbed her forehead. "I know I wasn't the best older sister, and I should have tried harder to have a relationship with Lauren and to get to know Noah. I have tremendous regrets about that now that she is gone." She bit her lip when it started to tremble. "But I'm not sure what she wants me to forgive her for?" She waved an arm around her. "For this? For becoming Amish? Or did she miss our relationship, even a little?" She dabbed at her eyes. "Forgive her for not attending our mother's funeral?"

Caroline needed to throw this woman a bone, even if she'd stolen the most precious part of hers and Abe's life. "Lauren had many regrets. In the beginning, it was about the life she'd led before she found a home here.

But as she grew in her relationship with the Lord, she told me that she had regrets about you too. She wanted you to be in Noah's life, but she'd ousted you because you didn't agree with her way of life. And, even though we believe in separation from the outside world, you were still her family. She talked often of ways to make things right between the two of you. But when you went to see Noah in the hospital nursery, you didn't visit her. She took that as a strong no, that you didn't want to be in her life."

Emily was quiet, her eyes moist. She looked a lot like Lauren, and Noah favored them both. Caroline's eyes grew moist, mostly from missing Lauren, not because she had a tremendous amount of sympathy for Emily.

"I assumed the baby would be in the room with Lauren. When I asked a nurse about Lauren and the baby, she said the baby was in the nursery because they were monitoring his heart rate. She assured me Noah would be fine, but I went to the nursery to see him, then I chickened out about seeing Lauren. I should have visited her, but I didn't understand your way of life." She locked eyes with Caroline. "I still don't. But she was my sister."

"You don't have to understand our way of life any more than we have to understand yours. But we coexist in a world where we are free to practice our beliefs however we see fit." She held Emily's gaze. "Do you believe in *Gott*?"

The woman hesitated for longer than Caroline was comfortable with. "Yes, I do," she finally said. "But I don't really know Him. I mean, I pray, but . . ."

This was the worst part of Caroline's nightmare

coming true, that Noah wouldn't have a solid faith-based rearing. But she bit her tongue.

"I've prayed so hard for God to give me and Dylan a baby. I've prayed for years. And we've been blessed with some wonderful children to care for during their times of need." She shook her head, her eyes still locked with Caroline's. "But why did He deny me a child all these years? Now, my sister is gone, and I have a child to raise, but it came with consequences, and I don't understand how God works."

Caroline was tempted to be honest with Emily, to tell her that her own faith had slipped due to all the praying she'd done over the years, begging for a child to love. But she chose not to. "We must accept *Gott's* will, whatever it might be." She cleared her throat before she stood up. "I'd like to spend time with Noah while I have a chance." Even though she didn't want to sound snarky, she knew she probably did.

Emily stood up too. "I have a few errands to run if you'd like for me to leave him here for a couple of hours."

Caroline put a hand to her chest. "*Ya, ya.* We would love that." She couldn't stop the smile that spread across her face.

"This really is going against what Dylan and I discussed, about letting Noah get used to us as a family unit before we allowed others into our circle." She hung her head, then looked back at Caroline. "He is going to scream and cry when I take him home with me, and it's going to be horrible."

Caroline lowered her eyes to the cool grass, wiggling her bare feet. "*Ya*, but we will return him to you as I know we are legally bound to do so." She looked up again. "But we will make this time we have with him special and do our best to encourage him to go with you without a fight."

Emily lowered her sunglasses. "Okay, I'll be back in a couple of hours."

After she left, Caroline eyed the buggy tethered outside the barn, then she looked at the trailer Abe used to carry large furniture deliveries, and she wondered just how far they could get with Noah. It was a silly thought. If they were going to kidnap Noah, they'd go by bus.

CHAPTER FIVE

Emily went to the bank, stopped for a fish sandwich, browsed in an Amish shop, then just drove around the area. Montgomery was quaint and definitely had a plentiful Amish population. There were lots of horses and buggies traveling the streets. Emily and Dylan had a Montgomery address but they lived on the outskirts of the main town.

She drove by a one-room schoolhouse and slowed down as she tried to picture Lauren living on a farm and Noah attending school only through the eighth grade. It felt surreal, and when she'd first found out about Lauren's living arrangements, she'd been angry. It seemed traitorous not to at least share her son with Emily. Looking back, Emily reminded herself that she could have tried harder, a thought that always led her back to regrets.

Now, it was time to go pick up Noah. She took deep breaths as she pulled into Caroline and Abraham's driveway. Emily would have to drag her son kicking and screaming back to a place he didn't consider home at all.

Why should he? Her heart hurt just thinking about it. She sat in the car for a minute before she got out and went to the door. All the windows were open, so they had to know she was there.

A large man, maybe in his mid-thirties, answered the door. He had a friendly face, and when he smiled, his cheeks dimpled just above his beard.

"You must be Abraham." Emily extended her hand.

After he shook it, still smiling, he said, "Welcome to our home."

Emily was surprised by the warm welcome since Caroline hadn't exactly rolled out the red carpet.

When Emily walked into the living room, Caroline was on the floor with Noah building a tower out of blocks. It was impossible not to notice the way Caroline's expression fell from a sense of complete joy to instant despair when she saw Emily. Noah didn't even look up, preoccupied with keeping the blocks balanced.

"Wow. That's a great building," Emily said as she tried to sound excited, knowing what was coming.

Caroline stood up and brushed the wrinkles from her black apron. "*Danki* for letting him stay awhile." She glanced down at Noah so lovingly that Emily was tempted to leave the child there. But she couldn't. He was her flesh and blood, her son. He would adjust, and it was just going to take time.

"Noah, it's time for you to go." Abraham spoke firmly, but there was a sadness in his expression that also tugged at Emily's heart. When Noah didn't acknowledge Abraham, the man spoke up again. "*Sohn*, it's time for you to go home."

Noah didn't look up as he placed another block on the structure. "I am home."

Emily sighed. "I knew this would be a bad idea," she said in a whisper to Caroline.

The two women stared at each other, then glanced at Noah.

"Maybe if he could come once a week to visit? We could promise him that and give him something to look forward to, *ya*?" Caroline smiled a little. Emily didn't want him to look forward to coming here weekly. She wanted him to adjust to his own new home.

"He's got to get used to us, to his new family. I feel like weekly visits would just make that harder." She rubbed her forehead, biting her lip, as she and Caroline edged away from Noah. "And you know he isn't going to want to leave, so it's going to be emotional for both of us when he throws a fit."

Caroline folded her hands in front of her, a blank expression on her face before she turned to Noah. "Let's pick up these blocks. It's time for you to go home now, Noah."

Even though she was trying to be firm, there was a tremble in Caroline's voice.

In one vicious swoop, Noah swung his arm and knocked down all the blocks, then ran toward the door, stopping at the doorsill.

"You don't *lieb* me anymore, Caroline!" Then he turned to Caroline's husband. "And you don't *lieb* me, Abraham!"

Noah covered his face, and as Emily's throat began to close, she swallowed back tears.

Caroline lowered herself to Noah's level and spoke to him in Pennsylvania Dutch. Emily had no idea what she said, but Noah hugged Caroline, and then he went to Abraham and the man scooped him up, kissed him on the forehead, and set him down.

Noah slowly shuffled toward the car, not looking back as he walked to the car.

"Please tell me that you didn't promise him we would come back next week. This is my fault, today. I shouldn't have brought him here." Emily shook her head.

"We'd like to disagree if that's all right with you. We are very glad you brought him here today." Caroline raised her chin as she blinked back tears. "There are two holes in our hearts." She reached into her pocket and took out an envelope. "I struggled whether or not to show you this. It's very personal, and it was intended for my eyes only. But, in light of everything that is going on, I feel I should give it to you. It's a letter Lauren left for me when she moved out of our home to her own house. Perhaps this will help you understand your sister, the person she'd grown to be."

Emily hesitated but took the letter. She turned around when she heard a car door slam.

"He's angry with us," Caroline said. "Hopefully, over time . . ." She shook her head and left the room.

Abraham muffled a cough with his hand. "It is difficult for us, but *Gott* will see us through this. *Gott* doesn't make mistakes, so there is a lesson to be learned here for all involved. But, whatever it is, sometimes it takes great pain and loss to allow us the freedom to be happy."

Emily didn't have a clue what he meant, but she

nodded and went to the car. Noah was already buckled up in the backseat. He didn't say a word on the way home.

Caroline lifted her head from where she'd had it buried in her pillow. She didn't want to talk, but when Abraham sat down on the bed, she knew he needed to talk. She sat up, blotted her eyes with a tissue, and waited for him to say something.

"The *Englisch* woman, she seems nice." He ran his hand the length of his beard, something he did when he was deep in thought. "And she seems to want what's best for Noah."

Caroline sat up and tucked one leg underneath her on the bed. "*Ya*, she and her husband seem nice. But they are not what is best for Noah. Lauren would have wanted him with us and for him to grow up practicing our ways." She found her husband's eyes. "You know that, Abe."

He lowered his head and sighed. "*Ya*, I'm just trying to make sense of it in a way that helps us accept what has happened is *Gott's* will." He scratched his cheek before he looked back at her. "What was the letter you gave her?"

Caroline laid a hand on her husband's leg. "Something Lauren wrote to me after she'd been baptized. I didn't show it to you because I felt it would be prideful." She blinked back tears as she recalled the letter. "She mostly thanked me for showing her the way to *Gott*. But we both know *Gott* led her to us. We only worked under

His directive. And, *ya*, the letter was to me, but I know her words were intended for you too."

"You two had a special relationship, and I recognize that. I just always wanted Lauren and the boy to be happy." Abraham placed a hand on top of hers.

"And they were," she said with a weak smile. "And, now they're gone."

"I sense the *Englisch* woman will let us see Noah and have a place in his life. She doesn't appear heartless to me."

"But it won't be the same. He will grow up watching television and with all the influences of the outside world. He'll drive a car, go to parties, and be faced with more temptations than we can imagine." Caroline sniffled. "I can only pray he will make wise choices."

Abraham pulled her close to him and kissed her on the forehead. "That's all we can do, *mei lieb* . . . pray."

Emily walked beside a very sad little boy all the way to the front door. She was happy to smell the aroma of freshly baked cookies and grateful she had a husband who enjoyed cooking and baking.

"I smell cookies." She closed the door behind her, but instead of heading to the kitchen, Noah went directly to his bedroom and closed the door.

"Maybe things will be better after he starts school," Dylan said after Emily told him about the past few hours. "I thought it was good that school was already out. I thought it would give him a chance to get used to us. But maybe it would have been better if he had kids to be around."

"Maybe. I'll try to arrange some play dates with mothers who have children around his age." She set her purse on the counter, then slid into a chair at the kitchen table. "Are we doing the right thing, Dylan?"

"Of course. You're his only family." He sat down beside her.

She slowly turned to him. "Or are we just selfishly wanting a child of our own so bad that we are taking him away from everything that's familiar? No matter what, it's obvious Caroline and her husband love Noah. We don't even know him."

"But we will learn to know and love him, Babe. We will be wonderful parents."

There was a desperateness in her husband's voice, an emotion Emily felt as well. But the day had taken a toll on her. Then she remembered the letter Caroline had given her. "I'm going to go change into some Capri pants and a T-shirt. I'll be back." She stood up and took her purse with her.

She sat down on her bed and pulled the letter from her bag with shaky hands. As she unfolded it, she wondered if she would feel better or worse after reading it. She also wondered why Caroline wanted to share it with her since she'd made it sound like it was very personal and only for Caroline to see.

Taking a deep breath, she read:

Dear Caroline,

It seems like I should be able to tell you all of this in person, but I'm afraid I won't convey my feelings as well verbally. I want to be sure you understand how I feel. As Noah and I pack up to leave your home—yours and Abe's—my mind wanders back to the person I used to be. I know Gott *led me to you. If not for your unselfish, loving ways, I don't know where Noah and I would have ended up. I was in such a bad way when we arrived. Little did I know that* Gott *had set me on a path that would lead to a journey of not only discovery but of redemption. But you were His instrument, Caroline. Without you, I'm not sure I would have made it. I would have botched up my life further and surely ruined Noah's. You taught me about true love, how to not only love others with all my heart but to trust in* Gott's *love in a way I'd never understood.*

I wish my sister could see the ways I have changed. I have drained the water under my bridge, but I fear Emily's reserve is still quite filled with bitterness. I pray for her every day. I thank you for stepping in as my sister, and I will never think of you as anything less. You and Abe are my family, and Noah and I are blessed to be able to say that.

Even though we are moving into our own home, we carry with us everything you have taught us. I'm so glad Noah will grow up in a community filled with love, faith, and family. My shortcomings brought us to you and Gott, *but without those painful steps on the wrong path, Noah might not have this blessed opportunity to be on the journey I know* Gott *chose for him.*

Love always,

Lauren, Your sister in Christ

Emily wasn't sure when she started crying, but when

she looked up and saw Noah standing in the doorway, there was no hiding her tears.

He was still wearing his suspenders and straw hat, and his puzzled expression was one of tense worry and concern as he stepped closer to her.

"You're crying," he said when he stopped about a foot in front of her.

"Yeah, I am." She sniffled, not knowing how to explain her feelings to a six-year-old. "But I will be okay."

"I'm sorry you're sad." He inched closer, his head tipped to one side as he frowned. "Did I make you cry?"

"No." She shook her head. "No, you didn't. You didn't do anything to make me cry."

As Noah stared at her, Lauren's words echoed in her mind. "Noah, I know that you love Caroline and Abraham very much. And I know you miss your mommy. But is there any way that you might be able to give us a chance at being your parents? Your mother was my sister, and Dylan and I want nothing more than to love you as our son for the rest of our lives."

His face shriveled up, and Emily worried he might cry, but he took a big breath and blew it out. "*Mei mamm* wants me to be with Caroline and Abe."

Emily pressed her lips together, wanting to shout out, "That's what Caroline told you to say." She couldn't wrap her mind around the possibility that Lauren spoke to her son in his dreams, not at his age anyway. Kids were resilient and over time, Noah would adjust and adapt to this new way of life.

"I know you might think that's what Mommy would

want, but I'm actually your family, your aunt. I want to raise you as if you were my very own son."

"I have a family." He spoke with maturity and calm that Emily didn't think she'd seen from a child his age. "I have Caroline and Abe, and I have Mattie and Chester, and Lloyd, David, Mary, Annie, Sarah, Marianne, Paul, Big Jim, and a lot of other people. I have a big family."

Emily was still trying to reconcile her own wants and needs, largely in contrast with her sister's letter and what Lauren wanted for her son.

As she gazed into Noah's eyes, he let her pull him into a hug. "I'm sorry you had to see me sad like this."

He laid his head on her shoulder. "It's okay. I'm sad too."

Emily thought her heart might crumble into pieces. As much as she wanted to honor her sister's wishes, selfishness won out.

I'm sorry, Noah. I can't give you up. Please grow to love us.

Then, as she mostly did in times of need, she begged God for Noah's love.

And keeping Noah away from Caroline and Abe was the only way that was going to happen.

Dinner that evening was somber, and despite Emily and Dylan's best efforts, Noah continued to look like he'd lost his best friend—or that his entire, very big family, had been stolen from him along with his mother.

Emily rubbed lotion on her hands as she and Dylan

got settled in bed. Her husband had just finished reading Lauren's letter to Caroline.

"How do you know she wrote the letter?" he asked.

"I recognize her handwriting." She closed the lid on the lotion and set it on the nightstand, then found her way into Dylan's arms. "Noah is too young to know what's best for him. A year from now, he will have been in school, made friends, and settled into our way of life. Maybe he'll want to be in Cub Scouts, and we should probably join a church. It'll all work out."

When Dylan didn't say anything, she wiggled out of his hold and looked into his eyes. "Say something." Her heart pounded in her chest. Had Lauren's letter caused him to reconsider the adoption? "We're right to have him. He's family."

Dylan stayed quiet as the lines on his forehead creased.

"Dylan," she said in a whisper. "Lauren isn't here, and we have to make the best decision for him. And *we* are best for him."

"You said we don't talk about God together. Maybe this is a time when we should. Are we doing the right thing in God's eyes?"

Emily bolted upright, her eyes burning with tears again. "Don't you do this. Don't you second-guess our only opportunity to have a child. We've tried and we've tried. And we'd loved so many children, and none of them were available for us to adopt." She crossed both hands over her heart. "We have enough love for a dozen children, and we're willing to bestow every ounce of it on that little boy. What if he is our only chance to be parents?"

Dylan's eyes watered. "Em . . ."

She covered her face with her hands and shook her head. "No, Dylan. No."

"It's not about us. It's about Noah," he said in a shaky voice.

"No, no, no." She spat the words at him as she violently shook her head before storming out of the room.

He is ours.

CHAPTER SIX

Caroline sat on the porch steps hand feeding one of the chickens that escapes the coop most mornings. She didn't hear Abe coming up on her from the backyard.

"Fence is repaired," he said as he made his way to the water pump.

Caroline tossed the last of the birdseed she had in her hand then leaned back on her palms.

"It's been over three weeks, Abe," she said when he sat down on the porch step beside her. "I guess Noah is settling in with his new family."

Her husband put an arm around her, and they quietly stared out across the pasture as the sun continued to rise in the distance. "I know your heart hurts, *mei lieb*. Mine does too. But we have to accept *Gott's* plan for Noah."

"I know." Caroline had finally stopped crying a week ago, but she'd also closed the door to Noah's bedroom and hadn't gone back inside. If only she could close the hole in her heart. There was an emptiness she couldn't fill. "I know you're right, but we helped raise that child. He's been a part of our lives for over six years."

"I guess the letter you gave Emily didn't sway her decision about Noah."

"*Nee*, I guess not." Caroline had hoped it would convey what Lauren would have wanted for Noah. "I know the feeling of a hollow womb, and it tends to override what might be right or wrong." She paused, considering the circumstances. "But if I were to conceive right now, even though we've been told that is impossible, it would not change *mei* feelings for Noah at all. I wonder if Emily could say the same thing. She wants a child, at any expense. I know those feelings, but this is Noah's home."

Abraham sighed. "We need a project, something to keep our minds busy. I've finished all the furniture I had orders for, and most of the repairs around here have been taken care of. We both miss the laughter, the boy's giggles, and his wonder at the simplest of things." He shook his head. "We need to keep busy as we heal."

Caroline didn't have much interest in a new project. She missed her best friend so much that it was a struggle just to get out of bed some mornings. And she felt like she'd failed Lauren even though she'd fought the English adoption system the best she'd known how.

She closed her eyes and silently prayed that Noah was happy.

~

Emily reached for Noah and Dylan's hand, and they each said their prayers aloud, the way they'd been doing for the past few weeks before every meal. And she'd found herself praying throughout the day. She and Dylan had also been praying aloud in bed before they went to sleep at night. Mostly Emily prayed that she'd feel some sort of peace. Thankfully, her husband didn't voice any doubts about Noah not staying with them, even though she was sure they were there.

Noah hadn't come around, and the child was miserable, despite the fact that they'd showered him with gifts —an above ground swimming pool, a small trampoline, a train set, and a host of other things that barely piqued his interest. He spent most days staring out the window hoping to catch sight of a buggy going by. Apparently, you couldn't buy a child's love. And Noah always prayed for Emily and Dylan to let him go home. It was the dagger in their hearts before the meal three times per day.

After several arguments, she and Dylan agreed not to take Noah to see Caroline and her husband. Dylan thought a visit would be good, but Emily didn't think so. She could tell that Noah's disposition was wearing on Dylan. He felt sorry for the boy and hated seeing him so unhappy. Emily convinced him that they just needed more time as a family.

"I need to go to Walmart in Bedford today." Emily dabbed her mouth with her napkin. We can get a jump on school supplies. Are you excited about starting school, Noah?" It was too soon to focus on school supplies, but she hoped maybe it would spark an interest for Noah.

He nodded, but with the enthusiasm of someone

being taken to jail. Ever since he'd caught Emily crying and hugged her, he hadn't thrown any fits or cried in front of them. She wondered, though, how hard he was crying on the inside. It didn't seem healthy for a boy his age to withhold his emotions, and Noah seemed to be doing it so as not to upset her.

It was early afternoon by the time she and Noah left for Walmart. It had taken some coaxing to get him to tag along. She and Dylan had only been giving him half of the chocolate balls at night, which usually worked, and Noah slept soundly. But on those nights when he was up and roaming, they usually gave in the following night and gave him a whole one. Last night, Noah had stumbled around his room mumbling to himself, but Emily had gotten him back to bed fairly easily.

"We can walk through the toy section and you can pick something out," she told Noah after Emily had stood in line and picked up a prescription that the doctor said might help Noah to sleep better. Even though the pediatrician said the herbs inside the chocolate ball wouldn't hurt Noah, he felt there were other options for him.

As had become his way, Noah tried to smile and nodded. But as they approached the aisle with the toys, they came face to face with Caroline. Emily felt a surge of panic that was soon justified as Noah ran to her and threw his arms around her waist. After Caroline had smoothed back his hair and kissed him on the forehead over and over again, she finally looked at Emily. The

Amish rarely showed any public emotion, but it hadn't mattered now.

Emily slowly approached them, still embracing. "I-I told Noah he could pick out a toy." She swallowed the lump building in her throat. "It's nice to see you Caroline." It was a lie she'd have to ask forgiveness for later.

"Take me home, Caroline," Noah said as he pressed his face into her black apron.

There was a sorrow in Caroline's eyes that Emily could relate to. "You have a home now, Noah, with Emily and Dylan," Caroline said.

Emily could see the woman's soul, the pain mirroring her own. She knew it took everything Caroline had to say what she did.

"Please, Caroline, please." Noah was starting to cry and clinging to Caroline the same way he'd done on that first day.

As Caroline latched on to Noah's arms and began prying him away from her, he only held tighter. "Noah, please," she said as her voice quivered.

"Stop." Emily laid a hand across her stomach and took a deep breath. "Noah, would you like to spend the night with Caroline and Abraham tonight?" She tried to keep her voice level, but it cracked just the same.

Noah quickly spun around and blinked his tear-filled eyes. "*Ya*. Can I?"

"Yes," Emily said barely above a whisper. "I can pick him up tomorrow afternoon, maybe around four, if you'd like." She locked eyes with Caroline.

"*Ya*, we'd like that very much." She leaned down to Noah. "*Sohn*, you can come and stay with us tonight, but tomorrow afternoon when Emily comes to pick you up, you will have to go without throwing a fit. Do you understand me?"

The word 'son' slid off of Caroline's tongue with an ease that brought forth a pain in Emily's chest. Noah nodded, his bright eyes twinkling as a smile filled his face. Emily, Dylan, and Noah had brief moments of joy, but Noah had never looked at her—not even once—the way he looked at Caroline now.

"Do you want to pick out a toy first?" Emily asked, but Noah quickly shook his head, keeping his eyes on Caroline.

"Wait here." Caroline pointed to the basket she was pushing before she walked closer to Emily. She put a hand on her arm. "Thank you for this," she said in a whisper. "We will do our very best to make the transition back to you as painless as possible tomorrow. We have missed him so much . . ." She brought a hand to her chest. For a moment Emily thought the woman might hug her, but she mouthed thank you again and went back to Noah.

Emily watched them walk away, both smiling and laughing. After they rounded the corner, Emily took the prescription she'd paid for out of the basket and stuffed it in her purse. She left the basket in the middle of the aisle, then left.

Caroline refused to focus on the fact that Noah would have to leave tomorrow. Instead, she was going to enjoy every moment with him.

"Look who I have!" she yelled as she walked into the house.

Noah ran to Abe's arms, and Caroline's husband lifted him high in the air. "Do I know you?" he teased.

"It's me, Noah!" The boy laughed when Abe swung him in circles, his feet flailing around as giggles once again filled their house.

For the rest of the day, the night, and the following day, their lives were back to normal. The new normal, without Lauren, but the closer it came to four o'clock, the more Caroline's stomach churned. Would it always be like this? Could time heal them all, and would Noah settle in at his new home? Or would Caroline feel like her heart was being ripped out every time they had to return Noah to Emily and Dylan?

She brushed the thoughts away, resolved to make each moment memorable, as the countdown to four o'clock continued.

Emily wrapped her arms around Dylan and kissed him on the cheek. "It will be awful. Are you sure you want to come?"

Her husband held her tightly. "Yeah. I don't want you going through that by yourself, and I should be there."

A half-hour later, they were in the car and on the way to Caroline and Abraham's. Neither one spoke, as if they were storing up energy for the emotional surge that was coming.

When they pulled into the driveway, Noah, Caroline, and Abraham were standing on the front porch, all with somber expressions. Emily was sure Noah had been given strict instructions not to fuss when they showed up, which tore at her heart again.

She stepped out of the car and met Dylan at the back of the minivan. She took out the small red suitcase Noah had shown up with. Dylan lifted out a larger one filled with some clothes and toys they'd gotten for Noah.

As they rounded the vehicle with the suitcases, Caroline and Abraham's jaws dropped. Noah scratched his cheek.

Dylan shook Abraham's hand as Emily introduced the two men, but all eyes were on the suitcases.

"Will you be letting us keep Noah for a while longer?" Caroline spoke in a hopeful, yet cautious voice.

"Forever," Emily said as a tear rolled down her cheek. She'd reread her sister's letter a dozen times the night before. "I might have failed Lauren, but I'm not going to fail her son or stand in the way of what she wanted for Noah. I'll talk to the adoption agency tomorrow and recommend that you and Abe be allowed to adopt him."

Caroline clamped a hand over her mouth as her husband blinked back tears.

"*Danki*," Abraham said when Caroline didn't seem to have any words, her eyes as moist as Emily's.

"We will provide a *gut* life for him," Caroline said through her tears.

"I know you will." Emily looked down at Noah, who stared at her. She lowered herself to eye level with him. "I hope that you will allow us to be a part of your life,

Noah. We wanted very much to be your parents." She glanced up at Caroline, then Abraham. "But, with your mother not here, I do believe she would want you to be with Caroline and Abraham." She lowered her head, trying desperately to gain control of her emotions. Dylan placed a hand on her shoulder before he squatted down also.

"But we'll still be your aunt and uncle, and I hope we will still have a place in your life."

Emily heard the shakiness in her husband's voice. He'd tried to be so strong for her the night before when they'd spent hours discussing Noah's future. But, now in the moment, he was struggling too.

When Emily glanced up at Noah, she was surprised when he laid a small hand against her cheek. "Don't be sad." Then he looked at Dylan. "Please don't be sad. I know I prayed to come home, but when I closed *mei* eyes at night in *mei* bed, I prayed that *Gott* would give you a *boppli* of your own."

"That means baby," Caroline said in a whisper.

Emily lowered her head again, fighting not to cry before she looked back at Noah. "I appreciate that Noah, but I don't think that's in God's plan for us."

With Dylan's help, Emily stood up, then she leaned down and kissed Noah on the cheek. The boy gently touched Emily's stomach and smiled. "*Mamm* said there is already a *boppli* in there."

Emily still wasn't sure she believed that Lauren spoke to Noah in his dreams, but a burst of adrenaline shot through every vein in her body. She looked at Caroline, who smiled.

"He's usually right." Caroline put a hand on Noah's head.

"Well, if that ever happened, you'd have a cousin." Emily was sure Noah couldn't make a prediction like that.

"Stop by whenever you'd like," Abraham said as they said their goodbyes. "You will always be welcome here, and we want you to be a part of Noah's life. Lauren would want that too."

Emily wasn't so sure about the last part, and she forced herself not to look back as they walked to the car. She waited until they went around the corner before she let the rest of the tears come pouring out. Dylan was quiet.

She finally blew her nose. "We did the right thing."

"Yes, we did."

They were quiet for a while. "Em . . ."

She turned to him, sniffling.

"You threw up yesterday morning."

"Yeah, I think it was just nerves." She shook her head. "So hard," she said in a whisper. But then she caught the underlying meaning in Dylan's question and she pulled her phone from her purse. She scrolled to the calendar and counted backward. She glanced at Dylan.

"There's no way . . ." She smiled. "Is there?"

He shrugged. "I don't know. You're the one with the calendar."

Instead of turning right toward home, Dylan made a left. "Only one way to find out. Up for a trip to Walmart? I think there are little tests for things like this?" He winked at her.

Emily had taken dozens of pregnancy tests over the years, but as she laid her hand across her stomach, she wondered if this test might be different from the others. With everything going on, she hadn't realized that she was three weeks late for her period. She'd never been that late before.

They ran into Walmart with the excitement of children Noah's age, and even the checkout clerk grinned as they paid for two tests. If the first one was positive, she wanted a second test to confirm the results.

But on the way home, Emily's stomach began to churn. Doubt crept in like a deceitful old friend giving hope, only to stab you in the back with disappointment. Dylan had grown quiet also.

Two tests later, Emily threw her arms around her husband's neck. God had answered their prayers. Maybe it was because they did the right thing, returning Noah to Caroline and Abe. Or, had they reached the necessary quota of prayers that was pleasing to God?

Emily's conclusion was they hadn't been ready before. Noah had inadvertently shown Emily and Dylan how to have a relationship with God, and how to have a better relationship as a couple through prayer. She'd always heard that things happened on God's timeframe. And this was her and Dylan's time now.

Thank you, God.

EPILOGUE

One year later . . .

Emily carried a casserole as she stepped into Caroline and Abe's house. Noah almost knocked her over when he ran into the living room. But it wasn't to see Emily. After bumping into her, Noah went to Dylan, leaned down, and looked at Larna in the baby carrier. They'd named her after Lauren and Noah, and the name also meant peace or harmony, both of which Emily and Dylan had found.

"She's bigger than she was two weeks ago." Noah gently touched Larna on the cheek, which caused her to smile.

"She's three months old today," Dylan said proudly.

Emily went into the kitchen. "I'm not sure this cooked long enough. We might want to put it in for another thirty minutes." She set the chicken and rice casserole on the stove before she hugged Caroline. They'd been meeting every two weeks ever since they'd left Noah with Caroline and Abe. Emily never wanted to replace Lauren in Caroline's memories, but in many ways, the women had become like sisters, and she'd shared precious recollections about Lauren with Emily.

After Noah had returned to Caroline and Abe, Emily and Dylan had continued praying aloud before meals and at bedtime together. Emily still wondered if they would have found their more meaningful relationship with God if not for Noah. They'd eventually found a church to attend. She knew she had much to learn, but she also knew that you were never too old to seek Him out.

She often recalled what Lauren wrote in her letter . . . *My shortcomings brought us to you and* Gott, *but without those painful steps on the wrong path, Noah might not have this blessed opportunity to be on the journey I know* Gott *chose for him.*

Emily knew she'd been blessed as well—with Dylan, Larna, Noah, Caroline, and Abe. Something she never wanted to take for granted.

THANK YOU!

To my wonderful readers,

Thank you for reading *An Amish Adoption.* I hope you enjoyed this story as much as I enjoyed writing it.

Turn the page for some authentic Amish recipes!

Also, all of my books are listed in the back.

Deepest Appreciation,
Beth

Classic Amish Apple Pie

Streusel:

1/3 cup granulated sugar
1/4 cup brown sugar
6 tablespoon flour
1 teaspoon ground cinnamon
1 teaspoon grated nutmeg
1 pinch salt

Filling:

1/2 cup (1 stick) butter, cold
1/2 cup walnuts or pecans, coarsely chopped
1 unbaked 10 inch pie shell
4 large Granny Smith apples, peeled & sliced, about 4 cups
7 tablespoons flour
1 cup granulated sugar
1/2 teaspoon cinnamon

1 egg
1 cup heavy whipping cream
1 teaspoon vanilla extract

Instructions:

In a bowl, mix the streusel ingredients, 1/3 cup sugar, 1/4 cup brown sugar, 6 tablespoons flour, 1 teaspoon cinnamon, nutmeg and salt.

Add the butter and cut with two knives until the mixture is crumbly; it should still have a dry look to it. Add the nuts then set aside.

Preheat oven to 350 degrees F.

Place apples in the pie shell.

In a small bowl, mix 1 cup sugar, 7 tablespoons flour, and 1 teaspoon cinnamon. Beat the egg in a medium bowl, and add the cream and vanilla.

Add the sugar mixture to the egg mixture and blend. Pour over the apples.

Bake for 1 hour in the lower one-third of the oven. After 20 minutes, sprinkle streusel over the top and continue baking approximately 40 minutes longer, or until the top puffs and is golden brown.

Chicken and Rice Casserole

3 boneless chicken breasts
1 ½ cups uncooked rice
½ cup chopped onion
3 T. butter or margarine
2 ½ cups water
1 tsp. salt
1 tsp. celery salt
¼ tsp. pepper
¼ tsp. paprika

Preheat oven to 350. Spray an 8 x 13-inch glass casserole dish with cooking spray and set aside. Saute rice and onions in butter until light brown, stirring constantly. Add water, salt, celery salt, pepper, and paprika, then mix well. Pour into casserole dish. Place chicken breasts on top of mixture. Cover tight with foil and cook for 1 hour and 30 minutes. When done, cut up chicken and mix with rice.

Chicken Noodle Soup

1 broiler/fryer chicken (3 to 4 lbs.) cut up
10 c. water
1 large carrot, sliced
1 large onion, sliced
1 celery rib, sliced
1 garlic clove, minced

1 bay leaf
1 t. dried thyme
1 t. salt
¼ t. pepper

Soup Ingredients:
2 large carrots, sliced
2 celery ribs, sliced
1 medium onion, chopped
2 c. egg noodles, uncooked
1 c. frozen peas
½ c. cut green beans, frozen

In a large soup kettle or Dutch oven, combine the first ten ingredients. Bring to a boil. Reduce heat; cover and simmer for 1 ½ to 2 hours or until the meat is tender.

Remove chicken and cool. Remove and discard skin and bones. Chop chicken and set aside. Strain broth, discarding vegetables and bay leaf. Return broth to the pan; add carrots, celery, and onion. Bring to a boil. Reduce heat; cover and simmer for 10 minutes or until the vegetables are tender.

Add noodles and chicken. Bring to a boil. Reduce heat; cover and simmer for 6 minutes. Stir in peas and beans. Cook for 2 to 4 minutes or until beans and noodles are tender. Yield: 6 to 8 servings.

Cinnamon Raisin Bread

2 c. warm water

- 2 packages (1/4 ounce each) active dry yeast
- 1 c. sugar, divided
- ¼ c. canola oil
- 2 tsp. salt
- 2 eggs
- 6 to 6 ½ c. all-purpose flour
- 1 c. raisins
- Extra canola oil
- 3 tsp. ground cinnamon

Using a large bowl, dissolve yeast in warm water. Add ½ cup sugar, oil, salt, eggs, and 4 cups flour. Beat until smooth. Stir in enough remaining flour until it forms a soft dough.

On a floured surface; knead until smooth and elastic, about 6 to 8 minutes. Place in a greased bowl, turning once to grease top. Cover and let rise in a warm place or until doubled, about 1 hour.

Punch dough down. Turn onto a lightly floured surface; divide in half. Knead ½ cup raisins into each; roll each portion into a 15x9-in. rectangle. Brush with additional oil. Combine cinnamon and remaining sugar; sprinkle to within ½ in. of edges.

Tightly roll up, jelly-roll styled, starting with a short side; pinch seam to seal. Place, seam side down, in two greased

9x4-in. loaf pans. Cover and let rise until doubled, about 30 minutes.

Preheat oven to 375. Brush with oil. Bake 45-50 minutes or until golden brown. Remove from pans and cool on wire racks. Yield – 2 loaves (16 slices each).

Meat Pie

2 1/2 pounds potatoes. Peeled and cut in half inch squares

2 pounds boneless chuck roast

Salt

Pepper

2 uncooked pie crusts. (Recipe below or can use frozen)

Place chuck roast in Dutch oven or similar size pot.

Add water to cover. Bring to a boil. Continue simmering until tender. (2 to 3 hours)

Boil potatoes until soft (about 20 minutes). Drain.

Cut cooked roast in cubes and mix with potatoes.

Salt and pepper to taste

Fill uncooked pie crust and cover with top crust. Score top of crust to vent

Bake at 350 degrees for 45 minutes. Serve with brown gravy.

Pie crust (makes two)

3 cups all purpose flour
4 teaspoons white sugar
2 teaspoons salt
1 cup vegetable oil
4 tablespoons milk

Mix together in large mixing bowl. Divide in half. Chill for 1 hour. Roll each crust out on wax paper. (Sprinkle flour on top before rolling).

Paprika Potatoes

¼ cup flour
¼ cup Parmesan cheese
1 Tbsp. paprika
¾ tsp. salt
1/8 tsp. garlic salt (or onion salt)
6 medium potatoes
vegetable oil or cooking spray

Put all the ingredients, except the potatoes, into a gallon-size plastic baggie. Shake until well blended. Wash the potatoes and cut them into small wedges. Add potato wedges to the bag until 1/3 full. Shake the bag to coat the potatoes. Place them on an oiled pan and repeat until all the potatoes are covered with the mixture. Bake at 350 for 1 hour.

ACKNOWLEDGMENTS

A huge thanks to my family and friends who have supported me on this amazing journey. Your love and encouragement has sustained me many times—especially during the revision process and when I'm up against a tight deadline.

To my husband, Patrick, thank you for putting up with this crazy author. I can't imagine my life without you in it, and I love you very much. You complete me.

Janet Murphy, we've worked together for over a decade. You grew into your position and trained yourself to be my most valued resource. Even more importantly, we have also nurtured a friendship that has become very important to me. Thank you for all you do to keep me sane and organized!

A big shout out to my agent, Natasha Kern. Thank you for being supportive of all my projects and a true advocate for my career. I appreciate your honesty, kindness, and friendship.

To my heavenly Father, You have blessed me more than I could have ever imagined or predicted. Thank You for placing these stories upon my heart. I hope I will continue to write books that entertain and glorify You.

ABOUT THE AUTHOR

Bestselling and award-winning author Beth Wiseman has sold over two million books. She is the recipient of the coveted Holt Medallion, a two-time Carol Award winner, and she has won the Inspirational Reader's Choice Award three times. Her books have been on various bestseller lists, including the ECPA (Evangelical Christian Publishers Association) and *Publishers Weekly*.

Beth and her husband are empty nesters enjoying country life in south central Texas. Visit her online at BethWiseman.com.

ALSO BY BETH WISEMAN

Daughters of the Promise

Plain Perfect

Plain Pursuit

Plain Promise

Plain Paradise

Plain Proposal

Plain Peace

Land of Canaan

Seek Me With All Your Heart

The Wonder of Your Love

His Love Endures Forever

Amish Secrets

Her Brothers Keeper

Love Bears All Things

Home All Along

Amish Journeys

Hearts in Harmony

Listening to Love

A Beautiful Arrangement

Contemporary Women's Fiction

The Promise

A July Bride

The House that Love Built

Need You Now

Surf's Up

A Tide Worth Turning

Message In A Bottle

The Shell Collector's Daughter

Christmas by the Sea

Collections

An Amish Christmas Bakery

An Amish Reunion

An Amish Homecoming

An Amish Spring

Amish Celebrations

An Amish Heirloom

An Amish Christmas Love

An Amish Home

An Amish Harvest

An Amish Year

An Amish Cradle

An Amish Second Christmas

An Amish Garden

An Amish Miracle

An Amish Kitchen

An Amish Wedding

An Amish Christmas

Healing Hearts

An Amish Love

An Amish Gathering

Summer Brides

Made in the USA
Middletown, DE
05 September 2020

17938735R00120